A RING OF BELLS

A RING OF BELLS

Poems of John Betjeman

INTRODUCED AND SELECTED

BY IRENE SLADE

Illustrations by
EDWARD ARDIZZONE

JOHN MURRAY

© Editorial text and selection by John Murray (Publishers) Ltd 1962

First published 1962
Reprinted 1964, 1967, 1972, 1974, 1978, 1986

Printed and bound in Great Britain
by The Bath Press, Avon
and published by
John Murray (Publishers) Ltd
50 Albemarle Street London W1X 4BD

Paperback 0 7195 0101 6

INTRODUCTION

For myself,
I knew as soon as I could read and write
That I must be a poet . . .

This is what John Betjeman wrote in his autobiographical poem *Summoned by Bells*, looking back on his childhood in Highgate. Yet how few people could ever say, reflecting in middle age, that they had done what they were going to do when they were seven! Seven-year-olds generally want to be engine drivers, space pilots, television stars, jockeys or any one of the countless other glamorous-sounding things that are fashionable at the time. But in the next few years—or months, or weeks—the ambition changes and in the end they grow up to be something quite different.

The rare exceptions are, of course, the infant prodigies whose talents are so great in infancy that there is no doubt about what they will become when they grow up—the young Mozart, the young Macaulay, the young Pope. With John Betjeman it wasn't like that. As a child he had ambition without the corresponding talent:

The gap between my feelings and my skill
Was so immense, I wonder I went on.

But he did go on; he had to express himself in words, however bad his verses were, and although he was no prodigy, he had something else. He had an extraordinary capacity for observation—of objects, scenes and people—and he was acutely sensitive to his surroundings. To him a house was not just a place with four walls and a roof; it was a living thing that had an atmosphere and character of its own; it could feel and think. As he became older he lost none of that sensitivity; it did not become hard and blunted as he grew up. When he did become a poet he remembered his impressions of childhood so clearly that they inspired much of his writing.

John Betjeman became a poet by perseverance and hard work; it was no easy thing for him. His school career was not brilliant—he was far too interested in church architecture and looking at old buildings to concentrate on his lessons properly. At Oxford he was equally carried away both by the atmosphere of the town, with its beautiful medieval colleges, and by the social life of the undergraduates. He left without taking a degree. Then followed a series of jobs as a schoolmaster, then as a journalist.

All this time he was practising writing. He sent his poems to magazines and had most of them rejected. Yet the more he failed the more he wrote, and however disheartened he became, he never gave up. But in those years, from seven to his early twenties, his powers as a writer were maturing, and eventually it became easier for him to express himself in words. As the words came more fluently, his own originality of thought and style developed.

In 1932, when he was twenty-four, he had his first volume of poems published. There were twenty in all, and the book was called *Mount Zion*. ('Hymn', 'Croydon' and 'Westgate-on-Sea', included in this book, are from *Mount Zion*.) After that, small volumes of his poems were published every few years, but his work made very little stir in the literary world. In fact, he remained comparatively unknown as a poet for about twenty years after the publication of *Mount Zion*, except for a small and faithful following of admirers who had recognized his gifts and originality from the very beginning.

It was not until the mid-fifties that things started to change and a wider reading public began to be aware of him. Each of his books of poetry had sold more copies than the one before, but in 1958 all his poems were gathered together into one book—*John Betjeman's Collected Poems*—and no one could possibly have foreseen what a sensational event the publication of this was to be.

Suddenly, almost overnight it seemed, John Betjeman had become the most popular poet of his time. *Collected Poems* sold out so quickly when it appeared that the publishers had to reprint it three times within a month. In the history of John Murray's nothing like it had been known since they published Byron's *Childe Harold* in 1812, when copies were sold to a clamouring crowd through the windows of the publisher's house in Albemarle Street! After their publication the demand for Betjeman's poems continued and has continued ever since, and his enormous popularity shows that many of the people who read him are people who would never normally look at a book of poetry at all. Why is this?

There are many reasons why John Betjeman's verse finds a ready response in so many people, but the two most important ones are these: his writing is direct and uncomplicated, and the things he writes about are the familiar objects and experiences common to most people. The rhythm of his verse, with its prose-like qualities of continuous narrative, is simple to follow:

> I remember the dread with which I at a quarter past four
> Let go with a bang behind me our house front door
> And, clutching a present for my dear little hostess tight,
> Sailed out for the children's party into the night . . .

and

> The sort of girl I like to see
> Smiles down from her great height at me.
> She stands in strong, athletic pose
> And wrinkles her *retroussé* nose.

and

> "Yes, the Town Clerk will see you." In I went.
> He was, like all Town Clerks, from north of Trent;
> A man with bye-laws busy in his head
> Whose Mayor and Council followed where he led.

Another quality in John Betjeman's writing that endears him to his readers is that his is a voice which, in the midst of this 'atomic age' of speed, mass-production and the glorification of material wealth, calls on people to pause and look back awhile on the good things of the past before they are all gone. To him, buildings and places are the things that most reflect the passing of time and the present-day rush towards ugliness. He looks back to the merits of Victorian architecture, at which it was once the fashion to sneer, with its red brick, lavish ornamentation and imitations of the medieval English Gothic style. He sees in it the work of people who really *cared* for what they were doing, and who had an artistic purpose to express. To him it represents the last comparatively tranquil period of British social history before the coming of twentieth-century industrialization with its cheap, shoddy buildings spreading like a plague across the landscape.

But John Betjeman's feeling for the Victorian age is not the dominant theme of all his poetry. He observes life in his own age and writes about it in a way that no one else has done. The mass-produced houses, factories, new towns—even the local gas-works—all have places in his verse, so have the people who live and work in them. He observes them all with compassion and understanding; he never writes in anger about what he sees.

In 1960 *Summoned by Bells*, John Betjeman's story of his early years up to the time of leaving Oxford, was published. When you read this poem in blank verse, you will see how many ideas, subjects and moods of his later verse are drawn from his childhood and school days. In fact the little boy of seven, tramping over Hampstead Heath with pencil and writing-pad, in search of inspiration, is very much present in everything Betjeman has ever written since. His capacity for original observation as a child, his loves, hates, fears, weaknesses and strengths are much the same now as they were then, and it is this which makes it possible for him to communicate his ideas with such ease and directness to other people, for in every human being of whatever age, the sensibilities of childhood lie only a little way beneath the surface of the protective covering of years.

In the present selection of John Betjeman's poems for young readers, I have chosen certain passages from *Summoned by Bells* which set the theme for the group of poems that follow, so you will find that each poem in a section relates in some way to what has been said in *Summoned by Bells*. These extracts, given in the same order as they come in the chapters of the book, without any cuts in the middle, are important because they describe places, people and ideas that had their being in the earlier part of this century. You may already be familiar with the world of gas lamps, carriages, early motor-cars and railway trains; you have probably experienced it in your reading—Wilkie Collins, Robert Louis Stevenson (*Dr. Jekyll and Mr. Hyde*), John Galsworthy, G. K. Chesterton, Sir Arthur Conan Doyle (the Sherlock Holmes stories) and many others. You may live in a town or village which still has Victorian lamp-posts or pillar-boxes, or has the kind of houses and shops that John Betjeman knew as a child. But if you live in a new town or a modern built-up area, John Betjeman's Victorian and Edwardian worlds may be new to you.

Read the poems aloud, either to yourself or to somebody else if you can. If you do not understand a poem at first reading, read it again, and yet again until its rhythm takes a hold of you and its words begin to call up images in your mind. Enjoy the sound and full flavour of words that may be new to you:

> the incumbent enjoying a supine incumbency—

or
> *Ausgang* we were out of love—
> *Und eingang* we are in.

—you can always look them up in the notes afterwards. If you have ever heard John Betjeman read his poems aloud you will notice how often he stops to explain them as he goes along. The notes here are at the back of the book so that they do not distract from your enjoyment of the poems as you first read them. A great scholar and writer, Sir Arthur Quiller-Couch, who, among other things, compiled the invaluable *Oxford Book of English Verse*, once advised young people on reading poetry: 'Just go on reading: the Prince has always to break through the briars to kiss the Sleeping Beauty awake . . . you are the Prince, and she is worth it.'

IRENE SLADE

POEMS OF CHILDHOOD

HERE on the southern slope of Highgate Hill
Red squirrels leap the hornbeams. Still I see
Twigs and serrated leaves against the sky.
The sunny silence was of Middlesex.
Once a Delaunay-Belleville crawling up
West Hill in bottom gear made such a noise
As drew me from my dream-world out to watch
That early motor-car attempt the steep.
But mostly it was footsteps, rustling leaves,
And blackbirds fluting over miles of Heath.
    Then Millfield Lane looked like a Constable
And all the grassy hillocks spoke of Keats.
Mysterious gravel drives to hidden wealth
Wound between laurels—mighty Caenwood Towers
And Grand Duke Michael's house and Holly Lodge.

    But what of us in our small villa row
Who gazed into the Burdett-Coutts estate?
I knew we were a lower, lesser world
Than that remote one of the carriage-folk
Who left their cedars and brown garden walls
In care of servants. I could also tell
That we were slightly richer than my friends,
The family next door: we owned a brougham
And they would envy us our holidays.
In fact it was the mother there who first
Made me aware of insecurity
When war was near: "Your name is German, John"—
But I had always thought that it was Dutch . . .
That tee-jay-ee, that fatal tee-jay-ee
Which I have watched the hesitating pens
Of Government clerks and cloakroom porters funk.
I asked my mother. "No," she said, "it's Dutch;
Thank God you're English on your mother's side."
O happy, happy Browns and Robinsons!

Safe were those evenings of the pre-war world
When firelight shone on green linoleum;
I heard the church bells hollowing out the sky,
Deep beyond deep, like never-ending stars,
And turned to Archibald, my safe old bear,
Whose woollen eyes looked sad or glad at me,
Whose ample forehead I could wet with tears,
Whose half-moon ears received my confidence,
Who made me laugh, who never let me down.
I used to wait for hours to see him move,
Convinced that he could breathe. One dreadful day
They hid him from me as a punishment:
Sometimes the desolation of that loss
Comes back to me and I must go upstairs
To see him in the sawdust, so to speak,
Safe and returned to his idolator.

Safe, in a world of trains and buttered toast
Where things inanimate could feel and think,
Deeply I loved thee, 31 West Hill!
At that hill's foot did London then begin,
With yellow horse-trams clopping past the planes
To grey-brick nonconformist Chetwynd Road
And on to Kentish Town and barking dogs
And costers' carts and crowded grocers' shops
And Daniels' store, the local Selfridge's,
The Bon Marché, the Electric Palace, slums
That thrilled me with their smells of poverty—
Till, safe once more, we gained the leafy slope
And buttered toast and 31 West Hill.
Here from my eyrie, as the sun went down,
I heard the old North London puff and shunt,
Glad that I did not live in Gospel Oak.

"A diamond," "A heart," "No trumps," "Two spades"—
Happy and tense they played at Auction Bridge:

Two tables in the drawing-room for friends
From terra-cotta flats on Muswell Hill
And nearer Brookfield Mansions: cigarettes
And 'Votes for Women' ashtrays, mauve and green.
I watched the players, happy to be quiet
Till someone nice was dummy who would talk—
A talk soon drowned . . . "If you'd finessed my heart
And played your diamond . . ." "If I'd had the lead
I might have done." "Well, length is strength, you know."
"Not when your partner's sitting on the ace."
Did they, I wonder, leave us in a huff
After those hot post-mortems? All I knew
Were silks and bits of faintly scented fur
On ladies vaguely designated 'aunts'
Who came on second Thursdays to At Homes.

    The sunlit weeks between were full of maids:
Sarah, with orange wig and horsy teeth,
Was so bad-tempered that she scarcely spoke;
Maud was my hateful nurse who smelt of soap
And forced me to eat chewy bits of fish,
Thrusting me back to babyhood with threats
Of nappies, dummies and the feeding bottle.
She rubbed my face in messes I had made
And was the first to tell me about Hell,
Admitting she was going there herself.
Sometimes, thank God, they left me all alone
In our small patch of garden in the front,
With clinker rockery and London Pride
And barren lawn and lumps of yellow clay
As mouldable as smelly Plasticine.
I used to turn the heavy stones to watch
The shiny red and waiting centipede
Which darted out of sight; the woodlouse slow
And flat; the other greyish-bluey kind
Which rolled into a ball till I was gone
Out of the gate to venture down the hill.

"You're late for dinner, John." I feel again
That awful feeling, fear confused with thrill,
As I would be unbuttoned, bent across
Her starchy apron, screaming "Don't—Maud—don't!"
Till dissolution, bed and kindly fur
Of agéd, uncomplaining Archibald.

*   *   *

GROUP LIFE: LETCHWORTH

Tell me Pippididdledum,
   Tell me how the children are.
Working each for weal of all
   After what you said.

Barry's on the common far
   Pedalling the Kiddie Kar.
Ann has had a laxative
   And Aluréd is dead.

Sympathy is stencilling
   Her decorative leatherwork,
Wilfred's learned a folk-tune for
   The Morris Dancers' band.

I have my ex-Service man and
   Mamie's done a lino-cut.
And Charlie's in the *kinderbank*
   A-kicking up the sand.

Wittle-tittle, wittle-tittle
   Toodle-oodle ducky birds,
What a lot my dicky chicky
   Tiny tots have done.

Wouldn't it be jolly now,
   To take our Aertex panters off
And have a jolly tumble in
   The jolly, jolly sun?

FALSE SECURITY

I remember the dread with which I at a quarter past four
Let go with a bang behind me our house front door
And, clutching a present for my dear little hostess tight,
Sailed out for the children's party into the night
Or rather the gathering night. For still some boys
In the near municipal acres were making a noise
Shuffling in fallen leaves and shouting and whistling
And running past hedges of hawthorn, spikey and bristling.

And black in the oncoming darkness stood out the trees
And pink shone the ponds in the sunset ready to freeze
And all was still and ominous waiting for dark
And the keeper was ringing his closing bell in the park
And the arc lights started to fizzle and burst into mauve
As I climbed West Hill to the great big house in The Grove,
Where the children's party was and the dear little hostess.
But halfway up stood the empty house where the ghost is
I crossed to the other side and under the arc
Made a rush for the next kind lamp-post out of the dark
And so to the next and the next till I reached the top
Where The Grove branched off to the left. Then ready to drop
I ran to the ironwork gateway of number seven
Secure at last on the lamplit fringe of Heaven.

Oh who can say how subtle and safe one feels
Shod in one's children's sandals from Daniel Neal's,
Clad in one's party clothes made of stuff from Heal's?
And who can still one's thrill at the candle shine
On cakes and ices and jelly and blackcurrant wine,
And the warm little feel of my hostess's hand in mine?
Can I forget my delight at the conjuring show?
And wasn't I proud that I was the last to go?
Too over-excited and pleased with myself to know
That the words I heard my hostess's mother employ
To a guest departing, would ever diminish my joy,
I WONDER WHERE JULIA FOUND THAT STRANGE, RATHER COMMON

LITTLE BOY?

CROYDON

In a house like that
　　Your Uncle Dick was born;
Satchel on back he walked to Whitgift
　　Every weekday morn.

Boys together in Coulsdon woodlands,
　　Bramble-berried and steep,
He and his pals would look for spadgers
　　Hidden deep.

The laurels are speckled in Marchmont Avenue
　　Just as they were before,
But the steps are dusty that still lead up to
　　Your Uncle Dick's front door.

Pear and apple in Croydon gardens
　　Bud and blossom and fall,
But your Uncle Dick has left his Croydon
　　Once for all.

INDOOR GAMES NEAR NEWBURY

In among the silver birches winding ways of tarmac wander
　And the signs to Bussock Bottom, Tussock Wood and Windy
　　　　　　　　　　　　　　　　　　　　　Brake,
Gabled lodges, tile-hung churches, catch the lights of our Lagonda
　As we drive to Wendy's party, lemon curd and Christmas cake.
　　Rich the makes of motor whirring,
　　Past the pine-plantation purring
　　　　Come up, Hupmobile, Delage!
　　Short the way your chauffeurs travel,
　　Crunching over private gravel
　　　　Each from out his warm garáge.

Oh but Wendy, when the carpet yielded to my indoor pumps,
     There you stood, your gold hair streaming,
     Handsome in the hall-light gleaming,
There you looked and there you led me off into the game of clumps.
     Then the new Victrola playing
     And your funny uncle saying
"Choose your partners for a tox-trot! Dance until it's *tea* o'clock!
     Come on, young 'uns, foot it featly!"
     Was it chance that paired us neatly,
     I, who loved you so completely,
You, who pressed me closely to you, hard against your party frock?

"Meet me when you've finished eating!" So we met and no one
                                                    found us.
Oh that dark and furry cupboard while the rest played hide and seek!
Holding hands our two hearts beating in the bedroom silence
                                                    round us,
     Holding hands and hardly hearing sudden footstep, thud and
                                                    shriek.
          Love that lay too deep for kissing——
          "Where *is* Wendy? Wendy's missing!"
          Love so pure it *had* to end,
     Love so strong that I was frighten'd
     When you gripped my fingers tight and
Hugging, whispered "I'm your friend."

Good-bye Wendy! Send the fairies, pinewood elf and larch tree
                                                    gnome,
     Spingle-spangled stars are peeping
     At the lush Lagonda creeping
Down the winding ways of tarmac to the leaded lights of home.
     There, among the silver birches,
     All the bells of all the churches
Sounded in the bath-waste running out into the frosty air.
     Wendy speeded my undressing,
     Wendy is the sheet's caressing
     Wendy bending gives a blessing,
Holds me as I drift to dreamland, safe inside my slumber-wear.

2

DISCOVERING POETRY

For myself,
I knew as soon as I could read and write
That I must be a poet. Even today,
When all the way from Cambridge comes a wind
To blow the lamps out every time they're lit,
I know that I must light mine up again.

My first attraction was to tripping lines;
Internal rhyming, as in Shelley's 'Cloud',
Seemed then perfection. 'O'er' and 'ere' and 'e'en'
Were words I liked to use. My father smiled:
"And how's our budding bard? Let what you write
Be funny, John, and be original."
Secretly proud, I showed off merrily.
But certain as the stars above the twigs
And deeply fearful as the pealing bells
And everlasting as the racing surf
Blown back upon itself in Polzeath Bay,
My urge was to encase in rhythm and rhyme
The things I saw and felt (I could not *think*).

And so, at sunset, off to Hampstead Heath
I went with pencil and with writing-pad
And stood tip-toe upon a little hill,
Awaiting inspiration from the sky.
"Look! there's a poet!", people might exclaim
On footpaths near. The muse inspired my pen:
The sunset tipped with gold St. Michael's church,
Shouts of boys bathing came from Highgate Ponds,
The elms that hid the houses of the great
Rustled with mystery, and dirt-grey sheep
Grazed in the foreground; but the lines of verse
Came out like parodies of *A & M*.

The gap between my feelings and my skill
Was so immense, I wonder I went on.
A stretch of heather seen at Haslemere

And 'Up the airy mountain' (Allingham)
Merged in the magic of my Highgate pen:

> When the moors are pink with heather
> When the sky's as blue as the sea,
> Marching all together
> Come fairy folk so wee.

My goodness me! It seemed perfection then——
The brilliance of the rhymes A B, A B!
The vastness and the daintiness combined!
The second verse was rather less inspired:

> Some in green and some in red
> And some with a violet plume,
> And a little cap on each tiny head
> Watching the bright white moon.

I copied out the lines into a book,
A leather-bound one given me for verse
And stamped with my initials. There it stood
On the first page, that poem—a reproach.
In later years I falsified the date
To make it seem that I was only seven,
Not eight, when these weak stanzas were composed.

The gap from feeling to accomplishment!
In Highgate days that gap was yawning wide,
But awe and mystery were everywhere,
Most in the purple dark of thin St. Anne's:
Down Fitzroy Park what unimagined depths
Of glade led on to haunts of Robin Hood
(Never a real favourite of mine).
A special Tube train carried Archibald
Northward to Merton, south to Millfield Lane.
A silver blight that made my blood run cold
Hung on a grey house by the cemetery—
So that for years I only liked red brick.
The turrets on the chapel for the dead
And Holly Village with its prickly roofs
Against the sky were terrifying shapes.

"Dong!" went the distant cemetery bell
And chilled for good the east side of the hill
And all things east of me. But in the west
Were health and sunshine, bumps on Hampstead Heath,
Friends, comfort, railways, brandy-balls and grass;
And west of westward, somewhere, Cornwall lay.

Once when my father took me to the Tate
We stood enraptured by 'The Hopeless Dawn',
The picture first to move me. Twenty times,
They told me, had Frank Bramley watched the flame
Expiring in its candlestick before
He put it down on canvas. Guttering there,
It symbolized the young wife's dying hope
And the old mother's—gazing out to sea:
The meal upon the table lay prepared
But no good man to eat it: through the panes,
An angry sea below the early light
Tossed merciless, as I had seen the waves
In splendid thunder over Greenaway
Send driftwood shooting up the beach as though
Great planks were light as paper. "Put it down!
Translate the picture into verse, my boy,
And here's your opening—

> Through the humble cottage window
> Streams the early dawn."

The lines my father gave me sounded well;
But how continue them? How make a rhyme?

> O'er the tossing bay of Findow
> In the mournful morn.

With rising hopes I sought a gazetteer—
Findochty, Findon, Finglas, Finistère—
Alas! no Findow . . . and the poem died.

*   *   *

GREENAWAY

I know so well this turfy mile,
    These clumps of sea-pink withered brown,
The breezy cliff, the awkward stile,
    The sandy path that takes me down

To crackling layers of broken slate
    Where black and flat sea-woodlice crawl
And isolated rock pools wait
    Wash from the highest tides of all.

I know the roughly blasted track
    That skirts a small and smelly bay
And over squelching bladder-wrack
    Leads to the beach at Greenaway.

Down on the shingle safe at last
    I hear the slowly dragging roar
As mighty rollers mount to cast
    Small coal and seaweed on the shore,

And spurting far as it can reach
    The shooting surf comes hissing round
To leave a line along the beach
    Of cowries waiting to be found.

Tide after tide by night and day
    The breakers battle with the land
And rounded smooth along the bay
    The faithful rocks protecting stand.

But in a dream the other night
    I saw this coastline from the sea
And felt the breakers plunging white
    Their weight of waters over me.

There were the stile, the turf, the shore,
The safety line of shingle beach
With every stroke I struck the more
The backwash sucked me out of reach.

Back into what a water-world
Of waving weed and waiting claws?
Of writhing tentacles uncurled
To drag me to what dreadful jaws?

PARLIAMENT HILL FIELDS

Rumbling under blackened girders, Midland, bound for
Cricklewood,
Puffed its sulphur to the sunset where that Land of Laundries stood.
Rumble under, thunder over, train and tram alternate go,
Shake the floor and smudge the ledger, Charrington, Sells, Dale
and Co.,
Nuts and nuggets in the window, trucks along the lines below.

When the Bon Marché was shuttered, when the feet were hot and
tired,
Outside Charrington's we waited, by the 'STOP HERE IF
REQUIRED'.
Launched aboard the shopping basket, sat precipitately down,
Rocked past Zwanziger the baker's, and the terrace blackish brown,
And the curious Anglo-Norman parish church of Kentish Town.

Till the tram went over thirty, sighting terminus again,
Past municipal lawn tennis and the bobble-hanging plane;
Soft the light suburban evening caught our ashlar-speckled spire,
Eighteen-sixty Early English, as the mighty elms retire
Either side of Brookfield Mansions flashing fine French-window fire.

Oh the after-tram-ride quiet, when we heard a mile beyond,
Silver music from the bandstand, barking dogs by Highgate Pond;
Up the hill where stucco houses in Virginia creeper drown—
And my childish wave of pity, seeing children carrying down
Sheaves of drooping dandelions to the courts of Kentish Town.

3

POEMS OF EARLY SCHOOL

O PEGGY PUREY-CUST, how pure you were:
     My first and purest love, Miss Purey-Cust!
Satchel on back I hurried up West Hill
To catch you on your morning walk to school,
Your nanny with you and your golden hair
Streaming like sunlight. Strict deportment made
You hold yourself erect and every step
Bounced up and down as though you walked on springs.
Your ice-blue eyes, your lashes long and light,
Your sweetly freckled face and turned-up nose
So haunted me that all my loves since then
Have had a look of Peggy Purey-Cust.

     Along the Grove, what happy, happy steps
Under the limes I took to Byron House,
And blob-work, weaving, carpentry and art,
Walking with you; and with what joy returned.
Wendy you were to me in *Peter Pan*,
The Little Match Girl in Hans Andersen—
But I would rescue you before you died.
And once you asked me to your house to tea:
It seemed a palace after 31—
The lofty entrance hall, the flights of stairs,
The huge expanse of sunny drawing-room,
Looking for miles across the chimney-pots
To spired St. Pancras and the dome of Paul's;
And there your mother from a sofa smiled.
After that tea I called and called again,
But Peggy was not in. She was away;
She wasn't well. *House of the Sleeping Winds*,
My favourite book with whirling art-nouveau
And Walter Crane-ish colour plates, I brought
To cheer her sick-bed. It was taken in.
Weeks passed and passed . . . and then it was returned.
Oh gone for ever, Peggy Purey-Cust!

And at that happy school in Byron House
Only one harbinger of future woe
Came to me in those far, sun-gilded days—
Gold with the hair of Peggy Purey-Cust—
Two other boys (my rivals, I suppose)
Came suddenly round a corner, caught my arms
And one, a treacherous, stocky little Scot,
Winded me with a punch and "Want some more?"
He grunted when I couldn't speak for pain.
Why did he do it? Why that other boy,
Who hitherto had been a friend of mine,
Was his accomplice I could not divine,
Nor ever have done. But those fatal two
Continued with me to another school—
Avernus by the side of Highgate Hill.

Let those who have such memories recollect
Their sinking dread of going back to school.
I well remember mine. I see again
The great headmaster's study lined with books
Where somewhere, in a corner, there were canes.
He wrapped his gown, the great headmaster did,
About himself, chucked off his mortar-board
And, leaning back, said: "Let's see what you know,
How many half-crowns are there in a pound?"
I didn't know. I couldn't even guess.
My poor fond father, hearing nothing, smiled;
The gold clock ticked; the waiting furniture
Shone like a colour plate by H. M. Brock . . .
No answer—and the great headmaster frown'd;
But let me in to Highgate Junior School.

*   *   *

AN INCIDENT IN THE EARLY LIFE OF EBENEZER JONES, POET, 1828

"WE were together at a well-known boarding-school of that day (1828), situated at the foot of Highgate Hill, and presided over by a dissenting minister, the Rev. John Bickerdike. . . .

We were together, though not on the same form; and on a hot summer afternoon, with about fifty other boys, were listlessly conning our tasks in a large schoolroom built out from the house, which made a cover for us to play under when it was wet. Up the ladder-like stairs from the playground a lurcher dog had strayed into the schoolroom, panting with the heat, his tongue lolling out with thirst. The choleric usher who presided, and was detested by us for his tyranny, seeing this, advanced down the room. Enraged at our attention being distracted from our tasks, he dragged the dog to the top of the stairs, and there lifted him bodily up with the evident intention—and we had known him do similar things—of hurling the poor creature to the bottom.

'YOU SHALL NOT!' rang through the room, as little Ebby, so exclaiming at the top of his voice, rushed with kindling face to the spot from among all the boys— some of them twice his age.

But even while the words passed his lips, the heavy fall was heard, and the sound seemed to travel through his listening form and face, as, with a strange look of anguish in one so young, he stood still, threw up his arms, and burst into an uncontrollable passion of tears.

With a coarse laugh at this, the usher led him back by his ear to the form; and there he sat, long after his sobbing had subsided, like one dazed and stunned."
From an account written in 1879 by Ebenezer's brother, Sumner Jones.

The lumber of a London-going dray,
The still-new stucco on the London clay,
Hot summer silence over Holloway.

Dissenting chapels, tea-bowers, lovers' lairs,
Neat new-built villas, ample Grecian squares,
Remaining orchards ripening Windsor pears.

Hot silence where the older mansions hide
On Highgate Hill's thick elm-encrusted side,
And Pancras, Hornsey, Islington divide.

June's hottest silence where the hard rays strike
Yon hill-foot house, window and wall alike,
School of the Reverend Mr. Bickerdike,

For sons of Saints, blest with this world's possessions
(Seceders from the Protestant Secessions),
Good grounding in the more genteel professions.

A lurcher dog, which draymen kick and pass
Tongue lolling, thirsty over shadeless grass,
Leapt up the playground ladder to the class.

The godly usher left his godly seat,
His skin was prickly in the ungodly heat,
The dog lay panting at his godly feet.

The milkman on the road stood staring in.
The playground nettles nodded "Now begin"—
And Evil waited, quivering, for sin.

He lifted it and not a word he spoke,
His big hand tightened. Could he make it choke?
He trembled, sweated, and his temper broke.

"YOU SHALL NOT!" clear across to Highgate Hill
A boy's voice sounded. Creaking forms were still.
The cat jumped slowly from the window sill.

"YOU SHALL NOT!" flat against the summer sun,
Hard as the hard sky frowning over one,
Gloat, little boys! enjoy the coming fun!

"GOD DAMNS A CUR. I AM, I AM HIS WORD!"
He flung it, flung it and it never stirred,
"You shall not!—shall not!" ringing on unheard.

Blind desolation! bleeding, burning rod!
Big, bull-necked Minister of Calvin's God!
Exulting milkman, redfaced, shameless clod,

Look on and jeer! Not Satan's thunder-quake
Can cause the mighty walls of Heaven to shake
As now they do, to hear a boy's heart break.

4

POEMS OF HOLIDAYS

COME, Hygiene, goddess of the growing boy,
    I here salute thee in Sanatogen!
Anaemic girls need Virol, but for me
Be Scott's Emulsion, rusks, and Mellin's Food,
Cod-liver oil and malt, and for my neck
Wright's Coal Tar Soap, Euthymol for my teeth.
Come, friends of Hygiene, Electricity
And those young twins, Free Thought and clean Fresh Air:
Attend the long express from Waterloo
That takes us down to Cornwall. Tea-time shows
The small fields waiting, every blackthorn hedge
Straining inland before the south-west gale.

The emptying train, wind in the ventilators,
Puffs out to Egloskerry to Tresméer
Through minty meadows, under bearded trees
And hills upon whose sides the clinging farms
Hold Bible Christians. Can it really be
That this same carriage came from Waterloo?
On Wadebridge station what a breath of sea
Scented the Camel valley! Cornish air,
Soft Cornish rains, and silence after steam . . .
As out of Derry's stable came the brake
To drag us up those long, familiar hills,
Past haunted woods and oil-lit farms and on
To far Trebetherick by the sounding sea.

Oh what a host of questions in me rose:
Were spring tides here or neap? And who was down?
Had Mr. Rosevear built himself a house?
Was there another wreck upon Doom Bar?
The carriage lamps lit up the pennywort
And fennel in the hedges of the lane;
Here slugs were crawling over slabs of slate;
Then, safe in bed, I watched the long-legg'd fly
With red transparent body tap the walls

And fizzle in the candle flame and drag
Its poisonous-looking abdomen away
To somewhere out of sight and out of mind,
While through the open window came the roar
Of full Atlantic rollers on the beach.

Then before breakfast down toward the sea
I ran alone, monarch of miles of sand,
Its shining stretches satin-smooth and vein'd.
I felt beneath bare feet the lugworm casts
And walked where only gulls and oyster-catchers
Had stepped before me to the water's edge.
The morning tide flowed in to welcome me,
The fan-shaped scallop shells, the backs of crabs,
The bits of driftwood worn to reptile shapes,
The heaps of bladder-wrack the tide had left
(Which, lifted up, sent sandhoppers to leap
In hundreds round me) answered "Welcome back!"

Along the links and under cold Bray Hill
Fresh water pattered from an iris marsh
And drowned the golf-balls on its stealthy way
Over the slates in which the elvers hid,
And spread across the beach. I used to stand,
A speculative water engineer—
Here I would plan a dam and there a sluice
And thus divert the stream, creating lakes,
A chain of locks descending to the sea.
Inland I saw, above the tamarisks,
From various villas morning breakfast smoke
Which warned me then of mine; so up the lane
I wandered home contented, full of plans,
Pulling a length of pink convolvulus
Whose blossoms, almost as I picked them, died.

Bright as the morning sea those early days!
Though there were tears, and sand thrown in my eyes.
And punishments and smells of mackintosh,

Long barefoot climbs to fetch the morning milk,
Terrors from hissing geese and angry shouts,
Slammed doors and waitings and a sense of dread,
Still warm as shallow sea-pools in the sun
And welcoming to me the girls and boys.

Wet rocks on which our bathing-dresses dried;
Small coves, deserted in our later years
For more adventurous inlets down the coast:
Paralysis when climbing up the cliff—
Too steep to reach the top, too far to fall,
Tumbling to death in seething surf below,
A ledge just wide enough to lodge one's foot,
A sea-pink clump the only thing to clutch,
Cold wave-worn slate so mercilessly smooth
And no one near and evening coming on—
Till Ralph arrived: "Now put your left foot here.
Give us your hand" . . . and back across the years
I swing to safety with old friends again.
Small seem they now, those once tremendous cliffs,
Diminished now those joy-enclosing bays.

*   *   *

SEASIDE GOLF

How straight it flew, how long it flew,
   It clear'd the rutty track
And soaring, disappeared from view
   Beyond the bunker's back—
A glorious, sailing, bounding drive
That made me glad I was alive.

And down the fairway, far along
   It glowed a lonely white;
I played an iron sure and strong
   And clipp'd it out of sight,
And spite of grassy banks between
I knew I'd find it on the green.

And so I did. It lay content
   Two paces from the pin;
A steady putt and then it went
   Oh, most securely in.
The very turf rejoiced to see
That quite unprecedented three.

Ah! seaweed smells from sandy caves
   And thyme and mist in whiffs,
In-coming tide, Atlantic waves
   Slapping the sunny cliffs,
Lark song and sea sounds in the air
And splendour, splendour everywhere.

TREBETHERICK

We used to picnic where the thrift
   Grew deep and tufted to the edge;
We saw the yellow foam-flakes drift
   In trembling sponges on the ledge
Below us, till the wind would lift
   Them up the cliff and o'er the hedge.
Sand in the sandwiches, wasps in the tea,
Sun on our bathing-dresses heavy with the wet,
Squelch of the bladder-wrack waiting for the sea,
Fleas round the tamarisk, an early cigarette.

From where the coastguard houses stood
   One used to see, below the hill,
The lichened branches of a wood
   In summer silver-cool and still;
And there the Shade of Evil could
   Stretch out at us from Shilla Mill.
Thick with sloe and blackberry, uneven in the light,
Lonely ran the hedge, the heavy meadow was remote,
The oldest part of Cornwall was the wood as black as night,
And the pheasant and the rabbit lay torn open at the throat.

But when a storm was at its height,
    And feathery slate was black in rain,
And tamarisks were hung with light
    And golden sand was brown again,
Spring tide and blizzard would unite
    And sea came flooding up the lane.
Waves full of treasure then were roaring up the beach,
Ropes round our mackintoshes, waders warm and dry,
We waited for the wreckage to come swirling into reach,
Ralph, Vasey, Alastair, Biddy, John and I.

Then roller into roller curled
    And thundered down the rocky bay,
And we were in a water-world
    Of rain and blizzard, sea and spray,
And one against the other hurled
    We struggled round to Greenaway.
Blessèd be St. Enodoc, blessèd be the wave,
Blessèd be the springy turf, we pray, pray to thee,
Ask for our children all the happy days you gave
To Ralph, Vasey, Alastair, Biddy, John and me.

EAST ANGLIAN BATHE

Oh when the early morning at the seaside
    Took us with hurrying steps from Horsey Mere
To see the whistling bent-grass on the leeside
    And then the tumbled breaker-line appear,
On high, the clouds with mighty adumbration
    Sailed over us to seaward fast and clear
And jellyfish in quivering isolation
    Lay silted in the dry sand of the breeze
And we, along the table-land of beach blown
    Went gooseflesh from our shoulders to our knees
And ran to catch the football, each to each thrown,
    In the soft and swirling music of the seas.

There splashed about our ankles as we waded
    Those intersecting wavelets morning-cold,
And sudden dark a patch of sea was shaded,
    And sudden light, another patch would hold
The warmth of whirling atoms in a sun-shot
    And underwater sandstorm green and gold.
So in we dived and louder than a gunshot
    Sea-water broke in fountains down the ear.
How cold the bathe, how chattering cold the drying,
    How welcoming the inland reeds appear,
The wood-smoke and the breakfast and the frying,
    And your warm freshwater ripples, Horsey Mere.

BESIDE THE SEASIDE

Green Shutters, shut your shutters! Windyridge,
Let winds unnoticed whistle round your hill!
High Dormers, draw your curtains! Slam the door,
And pack the family in the Morris eight.
Lock up the garage. Put her in reverse,
Back out with care, now, forward, off—away!
The richer people living farther out
O'ertake us in their Rovers. We, in turn,
Pass poorer families hurrying on foot
Towards the station. Very soon the town
Will echo to the groan of empty trams
And sweetshops advertise Ice Cream in vain.

Solihull, Headingley and Golders Green,
Preston and Swindon, Manchester and Leeds,
Braintree and Bocking, hear the sea! the sea!
The smack of breakers upon windy rocks,
Spray blowing backwards from their curling walls
Of green translucent water. England leaves
Her centre for her tide-line. Father's toes,
Though now encased in coloured socks and shoes

And pressing the accelerator hard,
Ache for the feel of sand and little shrimps
To tickle in between them. Mother vows
To be more patient with the family;
Just for its sake she will be young again.
And, at that moment, Jennifer is sick
(Over-excitement must have brought it on,
The hurried breakfast and the early start)
And Michael's rather pale, and as for Anne . . .
"Please stop a moment, Hubert, anywhere."

So evening sunlight shows us Sandy Cove
The same as last year and the year before.
Still on the brick front of the Baptist Church
SIX-THIRTY. PREACHER:—*Mr. Pentecost*—
All visitors are welcomed. Still the quartz
Glitters along the tops of garden walls.
Those macrocarpa still survive the gales
They must have had last winter. Still the shops
Remain unaltered on the Esplanade—
The Circulating Library, the Stores,
Jill's Pantry, Cynthia's Ditty Box (Antiques),
Trecarrow (Maps and Souvenirs and Guides).
Still on the terrace of the big hotel
Pale pink hydrangeas turn a rusty brown
Where sea winds catch them, and yet do not die.

The bumpy lane between the tamarisks,
The escallonia hedge, and still it's there—
Our lodging-house, ten minutes from the shore.
Still unprepared to make a picnic lunch
Except by notice on the previous day.
Still nowhere for the children when it's wet
Except that smelly, overcrowded lounge.
And still no garage for the motor-car.
Still on the bedroom wall, the list of rules:
Don't waste the water. It is pumped by hand.

Don't throw old blades into the W.C.
Don't keep the bathroom long and don't be late
For meals and don't hang swim-suits out on sills
(A line has been provided at the back).
Don't empty children's sand-shoes in the hall.
Don't this, Don't that. Ah, still the same, the same
As it was last year and the year before—
But rather more expensive, now, of course.
"Anne, Jennifer and Michael—run along
Down to the sands and find yourselves some friends
While Dad and I unpack." The sea! the sea!

On a secluded corner of the beach
A game of rounders has been organised
By Mr. Pedder, schoolmaster and friend
Of boys and girls—particularly girls.
And here it was the tragedy began,
That life-long tragedy to Jennifer
Which ate into her soul and made her take
To secretarial work in later life
In a department of the Board of Trade.
See boys and girls assembled for the game.
Reflected in the rock pools, freckled legs
Hop, skip and jump in coltish ecstasy.
Ah! parted lips and little pearly teeth,
Wide eyes, snub noses, shorts, divided skirts!
And last year's queen of them was Jennifer.
The snubbiest, cheekiest, lissomest of all.
One smile from her sent Mr. Pedder back
Contented to his lodgings. She could wave
Her little finger and the elder boys
Came at her bidding. Even tiny Ruth,
Old Lady D'Erncourt's grandchild, pet of all,
Would bring her shells as timid offerings.

So now with Anne and Michael see her stand,
Our Jennifer, our own, our last year's queen,
For this year's *début* fully confident.

"Get in your places." Heard above the waves
Are Mr. Pedder's organising shouts.
"Come on. Look sharp. The tide is coming in!"
"He hasn't seen me yet," thinks Jennifer.
"Line up your team behind you, Christabel!"
On the wet sea-sand waiting to be seen
She stands with Anne and Michael. Let him turn
And then he'll see me. Let him only turn.
Smack went the tennis ball. The bare feet ran.
And smack again. "He's out! Well caught, Delphine!"
Shrieks, cartwheels, tumbling joyance of the waves.
Oh Mr. Pedder, look! Oh here I am!
And there the three of them forlornly stood.
"You ask him, Jennifer." "No—Michael?—Anne?"
"I'd rather not." "Fains I." "It's up to you."
"Oh, very well, then." Timidly she goes,
Timid and proud, for the last time a child.
"Can *we* play, Mr. Pedder?" But his eyes
Are out to where, among the tousled heads,
He sees the golden curls of Christabel.
"Can *we* play, Mr. Pedder?" So he turns.
"*Who* have we here?" The jolly, jolly voice,
The same but not the same. "*Who* have we here?
The Rawlings children! Yes, of course, you may,
Join that side, children, under Christabel."
No friendly wallop on the B.T.M.
No loving arm-squeeze and no special look.
Oh darting heart-burn, *under Christabel!*

So all those holidays the bitter truth
Sank into Jennifer. No longer queen,
She had outgrown her strength, as Mummy said,
And Mummy made her wear these spectacles.
Because of Mummy she had lost her looks.
Had lost her looks? Still she was Jennifer.
The sands were still the same, the rocks the same,
The seaweed-waving pools, the bathing-cove,

The outline of the cliffs, the times of tide.
And I'm the same, of course I'm always ME.
But all that August those terrific waves
Thundered defeat along the rocky coast,
And ginger-beery surf hissed 'Christabel!'

Enough of tragedy! Let wail of gulls,
The sunbows in the breakers and the breeze
Which blows the sand into the sandwiches,
Let castles crumbling in the rise of tide,
Let cool dank caves and dark interstices
Where, underneath the squelching bladder-wrack,
Lurk stinging fin and sharp, marauding claw
Ready to pierce the rope-soled bathing-shoe,
Let darting prawn and helpless jelly-fish
Spell joy or misery to youth. For we,
We older ones, have thoughts of higher things.
Whether we like to sit with Penguin books
In sheltered alcoves farther up the cliff,
Or to eat winkles on the Esplanade,
Or to play golf along the crowded course,
Or on a twopenny borough council chair
To doze away the strains of *Humoresque*,
Adapted for the cornet and the drums
By the conductor of the Silver Band,
Whether we own a tandem or a Rolls,
Whether we Rudge it or we trudge it, still
A single topic occupies our minds.
'Tis hinted at or boldly blazoned in
Our accents, clothes and ways of eating fish,
And being introduced and taking leave,
'Farewell', 'So long', 'Bunghosky', 'Cheeribye'—
That topic all-absorbing, as it was,
Is now and ever shall be, to us—CLASS.

Mr. and Mrs. Stephen Grosvenor-Smith
(He manages a Bank in Nottingham)

Have come to Sandy Cove for thirty years
And now they think the place is going down.
"Not what it was, I'm very much afraid.
Look at that little mite with *Attaboy*
Printed across her paper sailor hat.
Disgusting, isn't it? Who *can* they be,
Her parents, to allow such forwardness?"

The Browns, who thus are commented upon,
Have certainly done very well indeed.
The elder children bringing money in,
Father still working; with allowances
For this and that and little income-tax,
They probably earn seven times as much
As poor old Grosvenor-Smith. But who will grudge
Them this, their wild, spontaneous holiday?
The morning paddle, then the mystery tour
By motor-coach inland this afternoon.
For that old mother what a happy time!
At last past bearing children, she can sit
Reposeful on a crowded bit of beach.
A week of idleness, the salty winds
Play in her greying hair; the summer sun
Puts back her freckles so that Alfred Brown
Remembers courting days in Gospel Oak
And takes her to the Flannel Dance to-night.
But all the same they think the place 'Stuck up'
And Blackpool, next year—if there *is* a next.

And all the time the waves, the waves, the waves
Chase, intersect and flatten on the sand
As they have done for centuries, as they will
For centuries to come, when not a soul
Is left to picnic on the blazing rocks,
When England is not England, when mankind
Has blown himself to pieces. Still the sea,

Consolingly disastrous, will return
While the strange starfish, hugely magnified.
Waits in the jewelled basin of a pool.

HUNTER TRIALS

It's awf'lly bad luck on Diana,
   Her ponies have swallowed their bits;
She fished down their throats with a spanner
   And frightened them all into fits.

So now she's attempting to borrow.
   Do lend her some bits, Mummy, *do*;
I'll lend her my own for to-morrow,
   But to-day *I*'ll be wanting them too.

Just look at Prunella on Guzzle,
   The wizardest pony on earth;
Why doesn't she slacken his muzzle
   And tighten the breech in his girth?

I say, Mummy, there's Mrs. Geyser
   And doesn't she look pretty sick?
I bet it's because Mona Lisa
   Was hit on the hock with a brick.

Miss Blewitt says Monica threw it,
   But Monica says it was Joan,
And Joan's very thick with Miss Blewitt,
   So Monica's sulking alone.

And Margaret failed in her paces,
   Her withers got tied in a noose,
So her coronets caught in the traces
   And now all her fetlocks are loose.

Oh, it's me now. I'm terribly nervous.
I wonder if Smudges will shy.
She's practically certain to swerve as
Her Pelham is over one eye.

*   *   *   *   *

Oh wasn't it naughty of Smudges?
Oh, Mummy, I'm sick with disgust
She threw me in front of the Judges,
And my silly old collarbone's bust.

5

POEMS OF PEOPLE

PERCIVAL MANDEVILLE, the perfect boy,
  Was all a schoolmaster could wish to see—
Upright and honourable, good at games,
Well-built, blue-eyed; a sense of leadership
Lifted him head and shoulders from the crowd.
His work was good. His written answers, made
In a round, tidy and decided hand,
Pleased the examiners. His open smile
Enchanted others. He could also frown
On anything unsporting, mean or base,
Unworthy of the spirit of the school
And what it stood for. Oh the dreadful hour
When once upon a time he frowned on me!

Just what had happened I cannot recall—
Maybe some bullying in the dormitory;
But well I recollect his warning words:
"I'll fight you, Betjeman, you swine, for that,
Behind the bike shed before morning school."
So all the previous night I spewed with fear.
I could not box: I greatly dreaded pain.
A recollection of the winding punch
Jack Drayton once delivered, blows and boots
Upon the bum at Highgate Junior School,
All multiplied by X from Mandeville,
Emptied my bladder. Silent in the dorm
I cleaned my teeth and clambered into bed.
Thin seemed pyjamas and inadequate
The regulation blankets once so warm.
"What's up?" "Oh, nothing." I expect they knew . . .

And, in the morning, cornflakes, bread and tea,
Cook's Farm Eggs and a spoon of marmalade,
Which heralded the North and Hillard hours
Of Latin composition, brought the post.

Breakfast and letters! Then it was a flash
Of hope, escape and inspiration came:
Invent a letter of bad news from home.
I hung my head and tried to look as though,
By keeping such a brave stiff upper lip
And just not blubbing, I was noble too.
I sought out Mandeville. "I say," I said,
"I'm frightfully sorry I can't fight today.
I've just received some rotten news from home:
My mater's very ill." No need for more—
His arm was round my shoulder comforting:
"All right, old chap. Of course I understand."

* * *

THE OLYMPIC GIRL

The sort of girl I like to see
Smiles down from her great height at me.
She stands in strong, athletic pose
And wrinkles her *retroussé* nose.
Is it distaste that makes her frown,
So furious and freckled, down
On an unhealthy worm like me?
Or am I what she likes to see?
I do not know, though much I care.
εἴθε γενοίμην . . . would I were
(Forgive me, shade of Rupert Brooke)
An object fit to claim her look.

Oh! would I were her racket press'd
With hard excitement to her breast
And swished into the sunlit air
Arm-high above her tousled hair,
And banged against the bounding ball
"Oh! Plung!" my tauten'd strings would call
"Oh! Plung! my darling, break my strings
For you I will do brilliant things."

And when the match is over, I
Would flop beside you, hear you sigh;
And then, with what supreme caress,
You'd tuck me up into my press.
Fair tigress of the tennis courts,
So short in sleeve and strong in shorts,
Little, alas, to you I mean,
For I am bald and old and green.

HOW TO GET ON IN SOCIETY

Phone for the fish-knives, Norman
    As Cook is a little unnerved;
You kiddies have crumpled the serviettes
    And I must have things daintily served.

Are the requisites all in the toilet?
    The frills round the cutlets can wait
Till the girl has replenished the cruets
    And switched on the logs in the grate.

It's ever so close in the lounge, dear,
    But the vestibule's comfy for tea
And Howard is out riding on horseback
    So do come and take some with me.

Now here is a fork for your pastries
    And do use the couch for your feet;
I know what I wanted to ask you—
    Is trifle sufficient for sweet?

Milk and then just as it comes dear?
    I'm afraid the preserve's full of stones;
Beg pardon, I'm soiling the doileys
    With afternoon tea-cakes and scones.

POT POURRI FROM A SURREY GARDEN

Miles of pram in the wind and Pam in the gorse track,
  Coco-nut smell of the broom, and a packet of Weights
Press'd in the sand. The thud of a hoof on a horse-track—
    A horse-riding horse for a horse-track—
    Conifer county of Surrey approached
  Through remarkable wrought-iron gates.

Over your boundary now, I wash my face in a bird-bath,
  Then which path shall I take? that over there by the pram?
Down by the pond! or—yes, I will take the slippery third path,
    Trodden away with gym shoes,
    Beautiful fir-dry alley that leads
  To the bountiful body of Pam.

Pam, I adore you, Pam, you great big mountainous sports girl,
  Whizzing them over the net, full of the strength of five:
That old Malvernian brother, you zephyr and khaki shorts girl,
    Although he's playing for Woking,
    Can't stand up
  To your wonderful backhand drive.

See the strength of her arm, as firm and hairy as Hendren's;
  See the size of her thighs, the pout of her lips as, cross,
And full of a pent-up strength, she swipes at the rhododendrons,
    Lucky the rhododendrons,
    And flings her arrogant love-lock
  Back with a petulant toss.

Over the redolent pinewoods, in at the bathroom casement,
  One fine Saturday, Windlesham bells shall call:
Up the Butterfield aisle rich with Gothic enlacement,
    Licensed now for embracement,
    Pam and I, as the organ
  Thunders over you all.

IN THE PUBLIC GARDENS

In the Public Gardens,
　　To the airs of Strauss,
Eingang we're in love again
When *ausgang* we were *aus.*

The waltz was played, the songs were sung,
　　The night resolved our fears;
From bunchy boughs the lime trees hung
　　Their gold electroliers.

Among the loud Americans
　　Zwei Engländer were we,
You so white and frail and pale
　　And me so deeply me.

I bought for you a dark-red rose,
　　I saw your grey-green eyes,
As high above the floodlights,
　　The true moon sailed the skies.

In the Public Gardens,
　　Ended things begin;
Ausgang we were out of love
　　Und eingang we are in.

A SUBALTERN'S LOVE-SONG

Miss J. Hunter Dunn, Miss J. Hunter Dunn,
Furnish'd and burnish'd by Aldershot sun,
What strenuous singles we played after tea,
We in the tournament—you against me!

Love-thirty, love-forty, oh! weakness of joy,
The speed of a swallow, the grace of a boy,
With carefullest carelessness, gaily you won,
I am weak from your loveliness, Joan Hunter Dunn.

Miss Joan Hunter Dunn, Miss Joan Hunter Dunn,
How mad I am, sad I am, glad that you won.
The warm-handled racket is back in its press,
But my shock-headed victor, she loves me no less.

Her father's euonymus shines as we walk,
And swing past the summer-house, buried in talk,
And cool the verandah that welcomes us in
To the six-o'clock news and a lime-juice and gin.

The scent of the conifers, sound of the bath,
The view from my bedroom of moss-dappled path,
As I struggle with double-end evening tie,
For we dance at the Golf Club, my victor and I.

On the floor of her bedroom lie blazer and shorts
And the cream-coloured walls are be-trophied with sports,
And westering, questioning settles the sun
On your low-leaded window, Miss Joan Hunter Dunn.

The Hillman is waiting, the light's in the hall,
The pictures of Egypt are bright on the wall,
My sweet, I am standing beside the oak stair
And there on the landing's the light on your hair.

By roads 'not adopted', by woodlanded ways,
She drove to the club in the late summer haze,
Into nine-o'clock Camberley, heavy with bells
And mushroomy, pine-woody, evergreen smells.

Miss Joan Hunter Dunn, Miss Joan Hunter Dunn,
I can hear from the car-park the dance has begun.
Oh! full Surrey twilight! importunate band!
Oh! strongly adorable tennis-girl's hand!

Around us are Rovers and Austins afar,
Above us, the intimate roof of the car,
And here on my right is the girl of my choice,
With the tilt of her nose and the chime of her voice,

And the scent of her wrap, and the words never said,
And the ominous, ominous dancing ahead.
We sat in the car park till twenty to one
And now I'm engaged to Miss Joan Hunter Dunn.

THE OLD LIBERALS

Pale green of the *English Hymnal*! Yattendon hymns
    Played on the *hautbois* by a lady dress'd in blue
    Her white-hair'd father accompanying her thereto
On tenor or bass-recorder. Daylight swims
    On sectional bookcase, delicate cup and plate
    And William de Morgan tiles around the grate
And many the silver birches the pearly light shines through.

I think such a running together of woodwind sound,
    Such painstaking piping high on a Berkshire hill,
    Is sad as an English autumn heavy and still,
Sad as a country silence, tractor-drowned;

For deep in the hearts of the man and the woman playing
    The rose of a world that was not has withered away.
Where are the wains with garlanded swathes a-swaying?
Where are the swains to wend through the lanes a-maying?
    Where are the blithe and jocund to ted the hay?
    Where are the free folk of England? Where are they?

Ask of the Abingdon bus with full load creeping
Down into denser suburbs. The birch lets go
But one brown leaf upon browner bracken below.
Ask of the cinema manager. Night airs die
To still, ripe scent of the fungus and wet woods weeping.
Ask at the fish and chips in the Market Square.
Here amid firs and a final sunset flare
Recorder and *hautbois* only moan at a mouldering sky.

LORD COZENS HARDY

Oh Lord Cozens Hardy
    Your mausoleum is cold,
The dry brown grass is brittle
    And frozen hard the mould
And where those Grecian columns rise
    So white among the dark
Of yew trees and of hollies in
    That corner of the park
By Norfolk oaks surrounded
    Whose branches seem to talk,
I know, Lord Cozens Hardy,
    I would not like to walk.

And even in the summer,
    On a bright East-Anglian day
When round your Doric portico
    Your children's children play
There's a something in the stillness
    And our waiting eyes are drawn
From the butler and the footman
    Bringing tea out on the lawn,
From the little silver spirit lamp
    That burns so blue and still,
To the half-seen mausoleum
    In the oak trees on the hill.

But when, Lord Cozens Hardy,
  November stars are bright,
And the King's Head Inn at Letheringsett
  Is shutting for the night,
The villagers have told me
  That they do not like to pass
Near your curious mausoleum
  Moon-shadowed on the grass
For fear of seeing walking
  In the season of All Souls
That first Lord Cozens Hardy,
  The Master of the Rolls.

EXCHANGE OF LIVINGS

Lines suggested by an advertisement in a
Broad Church newspaper

The church was locked, so I went to the incumbent
the incumbent enjoying a supine incumbency—
a tennis court, a summerhouse, deckchairs by the walnut tree
and only the hum of the bees in the rockery.
"May I have the keys of the church, your incumbency?"
"Yes, my dear sir, as a moderate churchman,
I am willing to exchange: light Sunday duty:
            nice district: pop 149: eight hundred per annum:
no extremes: A and M: bicyclist essential:
                          same income expected."

"I think I'm the man that you want, your incumbency.
Here's my address when I'm not on my bicycle,
            poking about for recumbent stone effigies—
14, Mount Ephraim, Cheltenham, Glos:
Rector St. George-in-the-Rolling Pins, Cripplegate:
non resident pop in the City of London:
eight fifty per annum (but verger an asset):
willing to exchange (no extremes) for incumbency,
similar income, but closer to residence."

DIARY OF A CHURCH MOUSE

Here among long-discarded cassocks,
Damp stools, and half-split open hassocks,
Here where the Vicar never looks
I nibble through old service books.
Lean and alone I spend my days
Behind this Church of England baize.
I share my dark forgotten room
With two oil-lamps and half a broom.
The cleaner never bothers me,
So here I eat my frugal tea.
My bread is sawdust mixed with straw;
My jam is polish for the floor.

Christmas and Easter may be feasts
For congregations and for priests,
And so may Whitsun. All the same,
They do not fill my meagre frame.
For me the only feast at all
Is Autumn's Harvest Festival,
When I can satisfy my want
With ears of corn around the font.
I climb the eagle's brazen head
To burrow through a loaf of bread.
I scramble up the pulpit stair
And gnaw the marrows hanging there.

It is enjoyable to taste
These items ere they go to waste,
But how annoying when one finds
That other mice with pagan minds
Come into church my food to share
Who have no proper business there.
Two field mice who have no desire
To be baptized, invade the choir.

A large and most unfriendly rat
Comes in to see what we are at.
He says he thinks there is no God
And yet he comes . . . it's rather odd.
This year he stole a sheaf of wheat
(It screened our special preacher's seat),
And prosperous mice from fields away
Came in to hear the organ play,
And under cover of its notes
Ate through the altar's sheaf of oats.
A Low Church mouse, who thinks that I
Am too papistical, and High,
Yet somehow doesn't think it wrong
To munch through Harvest Evensong,
While I, who starve the whole year through,
Must share my food with rodents who
Except at this time of the year
Not once inside the church appear.

Within the human world I know
Such goings-on could not be so,
For human beings only do
What their religion tells them to.
They read the Bible every day
And always, night and morning, pray,
And just like me, the good church mouse,
Worship each week in God's own house.

But all the same it's strange to me
How very full the church can be
With people I don't see at all
Except at Harvest Festival.

6

DISCOVERING ARCHITECTURE

ONE lucky afternoon in Chaundy's shop
  I bought a book with tipped-in colour plates—
'City of Dreaming Spires' or some such name—
Soft late-Victorian water-colours framed
Against brown paper pages. Thus it was
'Sunset in Worcester Gardens' meant for me
Such beauty in that black and shallow pool
That even to-day, when from the ilex tree
I see its shining length, I fail to hear
The all-too-near and omnipresent train.
The Founder's Tower in Magdalen still seems drowned
In red Virginia creeper, and The High
Has but one horse-tram down its famous length,
While a gowned Doctor of Divinity
Enters the porch of Univ.; Christ Church stairs
(A single column supporting the intricate roof),
Wallflowers upon the ruined city wall,
Wistaria-mantled buildings in St. John's—
All that was crumbling, picturesque and quaint
Informed my taste and sent me biking off,
Escaped from games, for Architecture bound.

  Can words express the unexampled thrill
I first enjoyed in Norm., E.E. and Dec.?
Norm., crude and round and strong and primitive,
E.E., so lofty, pointed, fine and pure,
And Dec. the high perfection of it all,
Flowingly curvilinear, from which
The Perp. showed such a 'lamentable decline'.
Who knew what undiscovered glories hung
Waiting in locked-up churches—vaulting shafts,
Pillar-piscinas, floreated caps.,
Squints, squinches, low side windows, quoins and groins—
Till I had roused the Vicar, found the key,
And made a quick inspection of the church?
Then, full of my discovery returned,
Hot from my bicycle to Gerald Haynes.

Much do I owe this formidable man
(Harrow and Keble): from his shambling height
Over his spectacles he nodded down.
We called him 'Tortoise'. From his lower lip
Invariably hung a cigarette.
A gym-shoe in his hand, he stood about
Waiting for misdemeanours—then he'd pounce:
"Who's talking here?" The dormitory quailed.
"Who's talking?" Then, though innocent myself,
A schoolboy hero to the dorm at last,
Bravely I answered, "Please, sir, it was me."
"All right. Bend over." A resounding three
From the strong gym-shoe brought a gulp of pain.
"I liked the way you took that beating, John.
Reckon yourself henceforth a gentleman."

Were those the words that made me follow him,
Waiting for hours in churches while he fixed
His huge plate camera up and, a black cloth
Over his bald head, photographed the font?
Was that the reason why the pale grey slides
Of tympana, scratch dials and Norfolk screens
So pleased me at his lectures? I think not:
Rather his kindness and his power to share
Joys of his own, churches and botany,
With those of us whose tastes he could inform.
He motor-bicycled his life away,
Looking for orchids in the Wytham Woods,
And Early English in Northamptonshire.
He was the giver: ours it was to take.

               The bindweed hung in leafy loops
                 O'er half a hundred hawthorn caves,
              For Godstow bound, the white road wound
                 In swirls of dust and narrow shaves,
              And we were biking, Red Sea troops,
                 Between the high cow-parsley waves.

Port Meadow's level green grew near
    With Wytham Woods and Cumnor Hurst:
I clicked my Sturmey-Archer gear
    And pedalled till I nearly burst—
And, king of speed, attained the lead
    And got to gushing Godstow first.

The skiffs were moored above the lock,
    They bumped each other side to side:
I boarded one and made her rock—
    "Shut up, you fool," a master cried.
By reed and rush and alder-bush
    See soon our long procession glide.

There is a world of water weed
    Seen only from a shallow boat:
Deep forests of the bladed reed
    Whose wolves are rats of slimy coat,
Whose yellow lily-blossoms need
    Broad leaves to keep themselves afloat.

A heaving world, half-land, half-flood;
    It rose and sank as ripples rolled,
The hideous larva from the mud
    Clung to a reed with patient hold,
Waiting to break its sheath and make
    An aeroplane of green and gold.

The picnic and the orchid hunt,
    On Oxey mead the rounders played,
The belly-floppers from the punt,
    The echoes that our shouting made:
The rowing back, relaxed and slack,
    The shipping oars in Godstow shade . . .

Once more we biked beside the hedge—
    And darker seemed the hawthorn caves
And lonelier looked the water's edge,
    And we were sad returning slaves
To bell and rule and smell of school,
    Beyond the high cow-parsley waves.

*　　*　　*

HYMN

The Church's Restoration
  In eighteen-eighty-three
Has left for contemplation
  Not what there used to be.
How well the ancient woodwork
  Looks 'round the Rect'ry hall,
Memorial of the good work
  Of him who plann'd it all.

He who took down the pew-ends
  And sold them anywhere
But kindly spared a few ends
  Work'd up into a chair.
O worthy persecution
  Of dust! O hue divine!
O cheerful substitution,
  Thou varnishéd pitch-pine!

Church furnishing! Church furnishing!
  Sing art and crafty praise!
He gave the brass for burnishing,
  He gave the thick red baize,
He gave the new addition,
  Pull'd down the dull old aisle,
—To pave the sweet transition
  He gave th' encaustic tile.

Of marble brown and veinéd
  He did the pulpit make;
He order'd windows stainéd
  Light red and crimson lake.
Sing on, with hymns uproarious,
  Ye humble and aloof,
Look up! and oh how glorious
  He has restored the roof!

AN ARCHÆOLOGICAL PICNIC

In this high pasturage, this Blunden time,
    With Lady's Finger, Smokewort, Lovers' Loss,
And lin-lan-lone, a Tennysonian chime
    Stirring the sorrel and the gold-starred moss,
Cool is the chancel, bright the altar cross.

Drink, Mary, drink your fizzy lemonade
    And leave the king-cups; take your grey felt hat;
Here, where the low-side window lends a shade,
    There, where the key lies underneath the mat,
The rude forefathers of the hamlet sat.

Sweet smell of cerements and of cold wet stones,
    Hassock and cassock, paraffin and pew;
Green is a light which that sublime Burne-Jones
    White-hot and wondering from the glass-kiln drew,
Gleams and re-gleams this Trans arcade anew.

So stand you waiting, freckled innocence!
    For me the squinch and squint and Trans arcade;
For you, where meadow grass is evidence,
    With flattened pattern, of our picnic made,
One bottle more of fizzy lemonade.

SUNDAY MORNING, KING'S CAMBRIDGE

File into yellow candle light, fair choristers of King's
    Lost in the shadowy silence of canopied Renaissance stalls
In blazing glass above the dark glow skies and thrones and wings
    Blue, ruby, gold and green between the whiteness of the walls
And with what rich precision the stonework soars and springs
    To fountain out a spreading vault—a shower that never falls.

The white of windy Cambridge courts, the cobbles brown and dry,
  The gold of plaster Gothic with ivy overgrown,
The apple-red, the silver fronts, the wide green flats and high,
  The yellowing elm-trees circled out on islands of their own—
Oh, here behold all colours change that catch the flying sky
  To waves of pearly light that heave along the shafted stone.

In far East Anglian churches, the clasped hands lying long
  Recumbent on sepulchral slabs or effigied in brass
Buttress with prayer this vaulted roof so white and light and strong
  And countless congregations as the generations pass
Join choir and great crowned organ case, in centuries of song
  To praise Eternity contained in Time and coloured glass.

THE TOWN CLERK'S VIEWS

"Yes, the Town Clerk will see you." In I went.
He was, like all Town Clerks, from north of Trent;
A man with bye-laws busy in his head
Whose Mayor and Council followed where he led.
His most capacious brain will make us cower,
His only weakness is a lust for power—
And that is not a weakness, people think,
When unaccompanied by bribes or drink.
So let us hear this cool careerist tell
His plans to turn our country into hell.

"I cannot say how shock'd I am to see
The *variations* in our scenery.
Just take for instance, at a casual glance,
Our muddled coastline opposite to France:
Dickensian houses by the Channel tides
With old hipp'd roofs and weather-boarded sides.
I blush to think one corner of our isle
Lacks concrete villas in the modern style.

Straight lines of hops in pale brown earth of Kent,
Yeomen's square houses once, no doubt, content
With willow-bordered horse-pond, oast-house, shed,
Wide orchard, garden walls of browny-red—
All useless now, but what fine sites they'd be
For workers' flats and some light industry.

"Those lumpy church towers, unadorned with spires,
And wavy roofs that burn like smouldering fires
In sharp spring sunlight over ashen flint
Are out of date as some old aquatint.
Then glance below the line of Sussex downs
To stucco terraces of seaside towns
Turn'd into flats and residential clubs
Above the wind-slashed Corporation shrubs.
Such Georgian relics should by now, I feel,
Be all rebuilt in glass and polished steel.

"Bournemouth is looking up. I'm glad to say
That modernistic there has come to stay.
I walk the asphalt paths of Branksome Chine
In resin-scented air like strong Greek wine
And dream of cliffs of flats along those heights,
Floodlit at night with green electric lights.
But as for Dorset's flint and Purbeck stone,
Its old thatched farms in dips of down alone—
It should be merged with Hants and made to be
A self-contained and plann'd community.
Like Flint and Rutland, it is much too small
And has no reason to exist at all.

"Of Devon one can hardly say the same,
But South-West Area One's a better name
For those red sandstone cliffs that stain the sea
By mid-Victoria's Italy—Torquay.
And South-West Area Two could well include
The whole of Cornwall from Land's End to Bude.

Need I retrace my steps through other shires?
Pinnacled Somerset? Northampton's spires?
Burford's broad High Street is descending still
Stone-roofed and golden-walled her elmy hill
To meet the river Windrush. What a shame
Her houses are not brick and all the same.

"Oxford is growing up to date at last.
Cambridge, I fear, is living in the past.
She needs more factories, not useless things
Like that great chapel which they keep at King's.
As for remote East Anglia, he who searches
Finds only thatch and vast, redundant churches.

"But that's the dark side. I can safely say
A beauteous England's really on the way.
Already our hotels are pretty good
For those who're fond of *very simple food*—
Cod and two veg., free pepper, salt and mustard,
Followed by nice hard plums and lumpy custard,
A pint of bitter beer for one-and-four,
Then coffee in the lounge a shilling more.
In a few years this country will be looking
As uniform and tasty as its cooking.
Hamlets which fail to pass the planners' test
Will be demolished. We'll rebuild the rest
To look like Welwyn mixed with Middle West.

"All fields we'll turn to sports grounds, lit at night
From concrete standards by fluorescent light:
And over all the land, instead of trees,
Clean poles and wire will whisper in the breeze.
We'll keep one ancient village just to show
What England once was when the times were slow—
Broadway for me. But here I know I must
Ask the opinion of our National Trust.
And ev'ry old cathedral that you enter
By then will be an Area Culture Centre.

Instead of nonsense about Death and Heaven
Lectures on civic duty will be given;
Eurhythmic classes dancing round the spire,
And economics courses in the choir.
So don't encourage tourists. Stay your hand
Until we've really got the country plann'd."

7

POEMS OF PLACES

WHEN I returned from school I found we'd moved:
"53 Church Street. Yes, the slummy end"—
A little laugh accompanied the joke,
For we were Chelsea now and we had friends
Whose friends had friends who knew Augustus John:
We liked bold colour schemes—orange and black—
And clever daring plays about divorce
At the St. Martin's. Oh, our lives were changed!
Ladies with pearls and hyphenated names
Supplanted simpler aunts from Muswell Hill:
A brand-new car and brand-new chauffeur came
To carry off my father to the Works.
                    Old Hannah Wallis left:
For years she'd listened to me reading verse;
Tons, if you added them, of buttered toast
Had she and I consumed through all the days
In happy Highgate. Now her dear old face,
Black bonnet, sniffs and comfortable self
Were gone to Tottenham where her daughter lived.

    What is it first breeds insecurity?
Perhaps a change of house? I missed the climb
By garden walls and fences where a stick,
Dragged on the palings, clattered to my steps.
I missed the smell of trodden leaves and grass,
Millfield and Merton Lanes and sheep-worn tracks
Under the hawthorns west of Highgate ponds.
I missed the trams, the few North London trains,
The frequent Underground to Kentish Town.
Here in a district only served by bus,
Here on an urban level by the Thames—
I never really liked the Chelsea house.
"It's simply sweet, Bess," visitors exclaimed,
Depositing their wraps and settling down
To a nice rubber. "So artistic, too."
To me the house was poky, dark and cramped,

Haunted by quarrels and the ground-floor ghost.
I'd slam behind me our green garden door—
Well do I recollect that bounding thrill!—
And hare to Cheyne Gardens—free! free! free!—
By Lawrence Street and Upper Cheyne Row,
Safe to the tall red house of Ronnie Wright.

Great was my joy with London at my feet—
All London mine, five shillings in my hand
And not expected back till after tea!
Great was our joy, Ronald Hughes Wright's and mine,
To travel by the Underground all day
Between the rush hours, so that very soon
There was no station, north to Finsbury Park,
To Barking eastwards, Clapham Common south,
No temporary platform in the west
Among the Actons and the Ealings, where
We had not once alighted. Metroland
Beckoned us out to lanes in beechy Bucks—
Goldschmidt and Howland (in a wooden hut
Beside the station): 'Most attractive sites
Ripe for development'; 'Charrington's for coal';
And not far off the neo-Tudor shops.
We knew the different railways by their smells.
The City and South reeked like a changing-room;
Its orange engines and old rolling stock,
Its narrow platforms, undulating tracks,
Seemed even then historic. Next in age,
The Central London, with its cut-glass shades
On draughty stations, had an ozone smell—
Not seaweed-scented ozone from the sea
But something chemical from Birmingham.
When, in a pause between the stations, quiet
Descended on the carriage we would talk
Loud gibberish in angry argument,
Pretending to be foreign.

*   *   *   *   *

All silvery on frosty Sunday nights
Were City steeples white against the stars.
And narrowly the chasms wound between
Italianate counting-houses, Roman banks,
To this church and to that. Huge office-doors,
Their granite thresholds worn by weekday feet
(Now far away in slippered ease at Penge),
Stood locked. St. Botolph this, St. Mary that
Alone shone out resplendent in the dark.
I used to stand by intersecting lanes
Among the silent offices, and wait,
Choosing which bell to follow: not a peal,
For that meant somewhere active; not St. Paul's,
For that was too well-known. I liked things dim—
Some lazy Rector living in Bexhill
Who most unwillingly on Sunday came
To take the statutory services.

A single bell would tinkle down a lane:
My echoing steps would track the source of sound—
A cassocked verger, bell-rope in his hands,
Called me to high box pews, to cedar wood
(Like incense where no incense ever burned),
To ticking gallery-clock, and charity bench,
And free seats for the poor, and altar-piece—
Gilded Commandment boards—and sword-rests
                                        made
For long-discarded aldermanic pomp.
A hidden organist sent reedy notes
To flute around the plasterwork. I stood,
And from the sea of pews a single head
With cherries nodding on a black straw hat
Rose in a neighbouring pew. The caretaker?
Or the sole resident parishioner?
And so once more, as for three hundred years,
This carven wood, these grey memorial'd walls

Heard once again the Book of Common Prayer,
While somewhere at the back the verger, now
Turned Parish Clerk, would rumble out "Amen."

*   *   *

SOUTH LONDON SKETCH, 1844

Lavender Sweep is drowned in Wandsworth,
  Drowned in jessamine up to the neck,
Beetles sway upon bending grass leagues
  Shoulder-level to Tooting Bec.
Rich as Middlesex, rich in signboards,
  Lie the lover-trod lanes between,
Red Man, Green Man, Horse and Waggoner,
  Elms and sycamores round a green.
Burst, good June, with a rush this morning,
  Bindweed weave me an emerald rope,
Sun, shine bright on the blossoming trellises,
  June and lavender, bring me hope.

WESTGATE-ON-SEA

Hark, I hear the bells of Westgate,
  I will tell you what they sigh,
Where those minarets and steeples
  Prick the open Thanet sky.

Happy bells of eighteen-ninety,
  Bursting from your freestone tower!
Recalling laurel, shrubs and privet,
  Red geraniums in flower,

Feet that scamper on the asphalt
  Through the Borough Council grass,
Till they hide inside the shelter
  Bright with ironwork and glass,

Striving chains of ordered children
    Purple by the sea-breeze made,
Striving on to prunes and suet
    Past the shops on the Parade.

Some with wire around their glasses,
    Some with wire across their teeth,
Writhing frames for running noses
    And the drooping lip beneath.

Church of England bells of Westgate!
    On this balcony I stand,
White the woodwork wriggles round me,
    Clock towers rise on either hand.

For me in my timber arbour
    You have one more message yet,
"Plimsolls, plimsolls in the summer,
    Oh goloshes in the wet!"

MARGATE, 1940

From out the Queen's Highcliffe for weeks at a stretch
I watched how the mower evaded the vetch,
So that over the putting-course rashes were seen
Of pink and of yellow among the burnt green.

How restful to putt, when the strains of a band
Announced a *thé dansant* was on at the Grand,
While over the privet, comminglingly clear,
I heard lesser 'Co-Optimists' down by the pier.

How lightly municipal, meltingly tarr'd,
Were the walks through the Lawns by the Queen's Promenade
As soft over Cliftonville languished the light
Down Harold Road, Norfolk Road, into the night.

Oh! then what a pleasure to see the ground floor
With tables for two laid as tables for four,
And bottles of sauce and Kia-Ora[1] and squash
Awaiting their owners who'd gone up to wash——

Who had gone up to wash the ozone from their skins
The sand from their legs and the Rock from their chins,
To prepare for an evèning of dancing and cards
And forget the sea-breeze on the dry promenades.

From third floor and fourth floor the children looked down
Upon ribbons of light in the salt-scented town;
And drowning the trams roared the sound of the sea
As it washed in the shingle the scraps of their tea.

     *   *   *   *   *

Beside the Queen's Highcliffe now rank grows the vetch,
Now dark is the terrace, a storm-battered stretch;
And I think, as the fairy-lit sights I recall,
It is those we are fighting for, foremost of all.

[1] Pronounced Kee-ora.

HENLEY-ON-THAMES

I see the winding water make
A short and then a shorter lake
    As here stand I,
    And house-boat high,
Survey the Upper Thames.
    By sun the mud is amber-dyed
    In ripples slow and flat and wide,
    That flap against the house-boat side
And flop away in gems.

In mud and elder-scented shade
A reach away the breach is made
    By dive and shout
    That circles out

To Henley tower and town;
And "Boats for Hire" the rafters ring,
And pink on white the roses cling,
And red the bright geraniums swing
In baskets dangling down.

When shall I see the Thames again?
The prow-promoted gems again,
As beefy ATS
Without their hats
Come shooting through the bridge?
And "cheerioh" and "cheeri-bye"
Across the waste of waters die,
And low the mists of evening lie
And lightly skims the midge.

WANTAGE BELLS

Now with the bells through the apple bloom
Sunday-ly sounding
And the prayers of the nuns in their chapel gloom
Us all surrounding,
Where the brook flows
Brick walls of rose
Send on the motionless meadow the bell notes rebounding.

Wall flowers are bright in their beds
And their scent all pervading,
Withered are primroses heads
And the hyacinth fading
But flowers by the score
Multitudes more
Weed flowers and seed flowers and mead flowers our paths
are invading.

Where are the words to express
      Such a reckless bestowing?
The voices of birds utter less
      Than the thanks we are owing,
      Bell notes alone
      Ring praise of their own
As clear as the weed-waving brook and as evenly flowing.

UPPER LAMBOURN

Up the ash-tree climbs the ivy,
      Up the ivy climbs the sun,
With a twenty-thousand pattering
      Has a valley breeze begun,
Feathery ash, neglected elder,
      Shift the shade and make it run—

Shift the shade toward the nettles,
      And the nettles set it free
To streak the stained Carrara headstone
      Where, in nineteen-twenty-three,
He who trained a hundred winners
      Paid the Final Entrance Fee.

Leathery limbs of Upper Lambourn,
      Leathery skin from sun and wind,
Leathery breeches, spreading stables,
      Shining saddles left behind—
To the down the string of horses
      Moving out of sight and mind.

Feathery ash in leathery Lambourn
      Waves above the sarsen stone,
And Edwardian plantations
      So coniferously moan
As to make the swelling downland,
      Far-surrounding, seem their own.

HERTFORDSHIRE

I had forgotten Hertfordshire,
    The large unwelcome fields of roots
Where with my knickerbockered sire
    I trudged in syndicated shoots;

And that unlucky day when I
    Fired by mistake into the ground
Under a Lionel Edwards sky
    And felt disapprobation round.

The slow drive home by motor-car,
    A heavy Rover Landaulette,
Through Welwyn, Hatfield, Potters Bar,
    Tweed and cigar smoke, gloom and wet:

"How many times must I explain
    The way a boy should hold a gun?"
I recollect my father's pain
    At such a milksop for a son.

And now I see these fields once more
    Clothed, thank the Lord, in summer green,
Pale corn waves rippling to a shore
    The shadowy cliffs of elm between,

Colour-washed cottages reed-thatched
    And weather-boarded water mills,
Flint churches, brick and plaster patched,
    On mildly undistinguished hills—

They still are there. But now the shire
    Suffers a devastating change,
Its gentle landscape strung with wire,
    Old places looking ill and strange.

One can't be sure where London ends,
  New towns have filled the fields of root
Where father and his business friends
  Drove in the Landaulette to shoot;

Tall concrete standards line the lane,
  Brick boxes glitter in the sun:
Far more would these have caused him pain
Than my mishandling of a gun.

NORFOLK

How did the Devil come? When first attack?
  These Norfolk lanes recall lost innocence,
The years fall off and find me walking back
  Dragging a stick along the wooden fence
Down this same path, where, forty years ago,
My father strolled behind me, calm and slow.

I used to fill my hand with sorrel seeds
  And shower him with them from the tops of stiles,
I used to butt my head into his tweeds
  To make him hurry down those languorous miles
Of ash and alder-shaded lanes, till here
Our moorings and the masthead would appear.

There after supper lit by lantern light
  Warm in the cabin I could lie secure
And hear against the polished sides at night
  The lap lap lapping of the weedy Bure,
A whispering and watery Norfolk sound
Telling of all the moonlit reeds around.

How did the Devil come? When first attack?
  The church is just the same, though now I know
Fowler of Louth restored it. Time, bring back
  The rapturous ignorance of long ago,
The peace, before the dreadful daylight starts,
Of unkept promises and broken hearts.

LAKE DISTRICT

'On their way back they found the girls at Easedale, sitting beside the cottage where they sell ginger beer in August.' (*Peer and Heiress*, by Walter Besant.)

I pass the cruet and I see the lake
   Running with light, beyond the garden pine,
     That lake whose waters make me dream her mine.
Up to the top board mounting for my sake,
For me she breathes, for me each soft intake,
     For me the plunge, the lake and limbs combine.
   I pledge her in non-alcoholic wine
And give the H.P. Sauce another shake.

Spirit of Grasmere, bells of Ambleside,
   Sing you and ring you, water bells, for me;
     You water-colour waterfalls may froth.
Long hiking holidays will yet provide
   Long stony lanes and back at six to tea
     And Heinz's ketchup on the tablecloth.

ESSEX

'The vagrant visitor erstwhile,'
   My colour-plate book says to me,
'Could wend by hedgerow-side and stile,
   From Benfleet down to Leigh-on-Sea.'

And as I turn the colour-plates
   Edwardian Essex opens wide,
Mirrored in ponds and seen through gates,
   Sweet uneventful countryside.

Like streams the little by-roads run
   Through oats and barley round a hill
To where blue willows catch the sun
   By some white weather-boarded mill.

'A summer Idyll Matching Tye'
    'At Havering-atte-Bower, the Stocks'
And cobbled pathways lead the eye
    To cottage doors and hollyhocks.

Far Essex,—fifty miles away
    The level wastes of sucking mud
Where distant barges high with hay
    Come sailing in upon the flood.

Near Essex of the River Lea
    And anglers out with hook and worm
And Epping Forest glades where we
    Had beanfeasts with my father's firm.

At huge and convoluted pubs
    They used to set us down from brakes
In that half-land of football clubs
    Which London near the Forest makes.

The deepest Essex few explore
    Where steepest thatch is sunk in flowers
And out of elm and sycamore
    Rise flinty fifteenth-century towers.

I see the little branch line go
    By white farms roofed in red and brown,
The old Great Eastern winding slow
    To some forgotten country town.

Now yarrow chokes the railway track,
    Brambles obliterate the stile,
No motor coach can take me back
    To that Edwardian 'erstwhile'.

HARROW-ON-THE-HILL

When melancholy Autumn comes to Wembley
  And electric trains are lighted after tea
The poplars near the Stadium are trembly
    With their tap and tap and whispering to me,
      Like the sound of little breakers
      Spreading out along the surf-line
When the estuary's filling
    With the sea.

Then Harrow-on-the-Hill's a rocky island
  And Harrow churchyard full of sailors' graves
And the constant click and kissing of the trolley buses hissing
    Is the level to the Wealdstone turned to waves
      And the rumble of the railway
      Is the thunder of the rollers
As they gather up for plunging
    Into caves.

There's a storm cloud to the westward over Kenton,
  There's a line of harbour lights at Perivale,
Is it rounding rough Pentire in a flood of sunset fire
    The little fleet of trawlers under sail?
      Can those boats be only roof tops
      As they stream along the skyline
In a race for port and Padstow
    With the gale?

A LINCOLNSHIRE TALE

Kirkby with Muckby-cum-Sparrowby-cum-Spinx
Is down a long lane in the county of Lincs,
And often on Wednesdays, well-harnessed and spruce,
I would drive into Wiss over Winderby Sluice.

A whacking great sunset bathed level and drain
From Kirkby with Muckby to Beckby-on-Bain,
And I saw, as I journeyed, my marketing done
Old Caistorby tower take the last of the sun.

The night air grew nippy. An autumn mist roll'd
(In a scent of dead cabbages) down from the wold,
In the ocean of silence that flooded me round
The crunch of the wheels was a comforting sound.

The lane lengthened narrowly into the night
With the Bain on its left bank, the drain on its right,
And feebly the carriage-lamps glimmered ahead
When all of a sudden *the pony fell dead*.

The remoteness was awful, the stillness intense,
Of invisible fenland, around and immense;
And out of the dark, with a roar and a swell,
Swung, hollowly thundering, Speckleby bell.

Though myself the Archdeacon for many a year,
I had not summoned courage for visiting here;
Our incumbents were mostly eccentric or sad
But—*the Speckleby Rector was said to be mad*.

Oh cold was the ev'ning and tall was the tower
And strangely compelling the tenor bell's power!
As loud on the reed-beds and strong through the dark
It toll'd from the church in the tenantless park.

The mansion was ruined, the empty demesne
Was slowly reverting to marshland again—
Marsh where the village was, grass in the Hall,
And the church and the Rectory waiting to fall.

And even in springtime with kingcups about
And stumps of old oak-trees attempting to sprout,
'Twas a sinister place, neither fenland nor wold,
And doubly forbidding in darkness and cold.

And down swung the tenor, a beacon of sound,
Over listening acres of waterlogged ground
I stood by the tombs to see pass and repass
The gleam of a taper, through clear leaded glass,

And such lighting of lights in the thunderous roar
That heart summoned courage to hand at the door;
I grated it open on scents I knew well,
The dry smell of damp rot, the hassocky smell.

What a forest of woodwork in ochres and grains
Unevenly doubled in diamonded panes,
And over the plaster, so textured with time,
Sweet discoloration of umber and lime.

The candles ensconced on each high panelled pew
Brought the caverns of brass-studded baize into view,
But the roof and its rafters were lost to the sight
As they soared to the dark of the Lincolnshire night:

And high from the chancel arch paused to look down
A sign-painter's beasts in their fight for the Crown,
While massive, impressive, and still as the grave
A three-decker pulpit frowned over the nave.

Shall I ever forget what a stillness was there
When the bell ceased its tolling and thinned on the air?
Then an opening door showed a long pair of hands
And the Rector himself in his gown and his bands.

*   *   *   *   *

Such a fell Visitation I shall not forget,
Such a rush through the dark, that I rush through it yet,
And I pray, as the bells ring o'er fenland and hill,
That the Speckleby acres be tenantless still.

8

LATER SCHOOL

LUXURIATING backwards in the bath,
I swish the warmer water round my legs
Towards my shoulders, and the waves of heat
Bring those five years of Marlborough through to me,
In comfortable retrospect: 'Thank God
I'll never have to go through them again.'
As with my toes I reach towards the tap
And turn it to a trickle, stealing warm
About my tender person, comes a voice,
An inner voice that calls, 'Be fair! be fair!
It was not quite as awful as you think.'
In steam like this the changing-room was bathed;
Pink bodies splashed hot water on themselves
After the wonderful release from games,
When Atherton would lead the songs we sang.
I see the tall Memorial Reading Room,
Which smelt of boots and socks and water-pipes,
Its deaf invigilator on his throne—
"Do you tickle your arse with a feather, Mr. Purdick?"
"What?"
"Particularly nasty weather, Mr. Purdick!"
"Oh."

And, as the water cools, the Marlborough terms
Form into seasons. Winter starts us off,
Lasting two years, for we were new boys twice—
Once in a junior, then a senior house.
Spring has its love and summer has its art:
It is the winter that remains with me,
Black as our college suits, as cold and thin.

Doom! Shivering doom! Clutching a leather grip
Containing things for the first night of term—
House-slippers, sponge-bag, pyjams, Common Prayer,
My health certificate, photographs of home
(Where were my bike, my playbox and my trunk?)—

I walked with strangers down the hill to school.
The town's first gaslights twinkled in the cold.
Deserted by the coaches, poorly served
By railway, Marlborough was a lonely place;
The old Bath Road, in chalky whiteness, raised
Occasional clouds of dust as motors passed.

       *   *   *   *   *

There was a building known as Upper School
(Abolished now, thank God, and all its ways),
An eighteen-fifty warehouse smelling strong
Of bat-oil, biscuits, sweat and rotten fruit.
The corporate life of which the bishop spoke,
At any rate among the junior boys,
Went on within its echoing whitewashed walls.

Great were the ranks and privileges there:
Four captains ruled, selected for their brawn
And skill at games; and how we reverenced them!
Twelve friends they chose as brawny as themselves.
'Big Fire' we called them; lording it they sat
In huge armchairs beside the warming flames
Or played at indoor hockey in the space
Reserved for them. The rest of us would sit
Crowded on benches round another grate.

Before the master came for evening prep
The captains entered at official pace
And, walking down the alley-way of desks,
Beat on their level lids with supple canes.
This was the sign for new boys to arise,
To pick up paper, apple-cores and darts
And fill huge baskets with the muck they found;
Then, wiping hands upon grey handkerchiefs
And trousers, settle down to Latin prose.

Upper School captains had the power to beat:
Maximum six strokes, usually three.
My frequent crime was far too many books,
So that my desk lid would not shut at all:
"Come to Big Fire then, Betjeman, after prep."
I tried to concentrate on delicate points—
Ut, whether final or consecutive?
(Oh happy private-school days when I knew!)—
While all the time I thought of pain to come.
Swift after prep all raced towards 'Big Fire',
Giving the captain space to swing his cane:
"*One*," they would shout and downward came the blow;
"*Two*" (rather louder); then, exultant, "*Three!*"
And some in ecstasy would bellow "*Four*."
These casual beatings brought us no disgrace,
Rather a kind of glory. In the dorm,
Comparing bruises, other boys could show
Far worse ones that the beaks and prefects made.

No, Upper School's most terrible disgrace
Involved a very different sort of pain.
Our discontents and enmities arose
Somewhere about the seventh week of term:
The holidays too far off to count the days
Till our release, the weeks behind, a blank.
"Haven't you heard?" said D. C. Wilkinson.
"Angus is to be basketed tonight."
Why Angus . . . ? Never mind. The victim's found.
Perhaps he sported coloured socks too soon,
Perhaps he smarmed his hair with scented oil,
Perhaps he was 'immoral' or a thief.
We did not mind the cause: for Angus now
The game was up. His friends deserted him,
And after his disgrace they'd stay away
For fear of being basketed themselves.
"*By* the boys, *for* the boys. The boys know best.

Leave it to them to pick the rotters out
With that rough justice decent schoolboys know."
And at the end of term the victim left—
Never to wear an Old Marlburian tie

   In quieter tones we asked in Hall that night
Neighbours to pass the marge; the piles of bread
Lay in uneaten slices with the jam.
Too thrilled to eat we raced across the court
Under the frosty stars to Upper School.
Elaborately easy at his desk
Sat Angus, glancing through *The Autocar*.
Fellows walked past him trying to make it look
As if they didn't know his coming fate,
Though the boy's body called "Unclean! Unclean!"
And all of us felt goody-goody-good,
Nice wholesome boys who never sinned at all.
At ten to seven 'Big Fire' came marching in
Unsmiling, while the captains stayed outside
(For this was 'unofficial'). Twelve to one:
What chance had Angus? They surrounded him,
Pulled off his coat and trousers, socks and shoes
And, wretched in his shirt, they hoisted him
Into the huge waste-paper basket; then
Poured ink and treacle on his head. With ropes
They strung the basket up among the beams,
And as he soared I only saw his eyes
Look through the slats at us who watched below.

Seven. "It's prep." They let the basket down
And Angus struggled out. "Left! Right! Left! Right!"
We stamped and called as, stained and pale, he strode
Down the long alley-way between the desks,
Holding his trousers, coat and pointed shoes.
"You're for it next," said H. J. Anderson.

"I'm not." "You are. I've heard." So all that term
And three terms afterwards I crept about,
Avoiding public gaze. I kept my books
Down in the basement where the boot-hole was
And by its fishtail gas-jet nursed my fear.

9

GROWING UP

DEAR lanes of Cornwall! With a one-inch map,
A bicycle and well-worn *Little Guide*,
Those were the years I used to ride for miles
To far-off churches. One of them that year
So worked on me that, if my life was changed,
I owe it to St. Ervan and his priest
In their small hollow deep in sycamores.
The time was tea-time, calm free-wheeling time,
When from slashed tree-tops in the combe below
I heard a bell-note floating to the sun;
It gave significance to lichened stone
And large red admirals with outspread wings
Basking on buddleia. So, casting down
In the cool shade of interlacing boughs,
I found St. Ervan's partly ruined church.
Its bearded Rector, holding in one hand
A gong-stick, in the other hand a book,
Struck, while he read, a heavy-sounding bell,
Hung from an elm bough by the churchyard gate.
"Better come in. It's time for Evensong."

    There wasn't much to see, there wasn't much
The *Little Guide* could say about the church.
Holy and small and heavily restored,
It held me for the length of Evensong,
Said rapidly among discoloured walls,
Impatient of my diffident response.
"Better come in and have a cup of tea."
The Rectory was large, uncarpeted;
Books and oil-lamps and papers were about;
The study's pale green walls were mapped with damp;
The pitch-pine doors and window-frames were cracked;
Loose noisy tiles along the passages
Led to a waste of barely furnished rooms:
Clearly the Rector lived here all alone.

He talked of poetry and Cornish saints;
He kept an apiary and a cow;
He asked me which church service I liked best—
I told him Evensong . . . "And I suppose
You think religion's mostly singing hymns
And feeling warm and comfortable inside?"
And he was right: most certainly I did.
"Borrow this book and come to tea again."
With Arthur Machen's *Secret Glory* stuffed
Into my blazer pocket, up the hill
On to St. Merryn, down to Padstow Quay
In time for the last ferry back to Rock,
I bicycled—and found Trebetherick
A worldly contrast with my afternoon.

I would not care to read that book again.
It so exactly mingled with the mood
Of those impressionable years, that now
I might be disillusioned. There were laughs
At public schools, at chapel services,
At masters who were still 'big boys at heart'—
While all the time the author's hero knew
A Secret Glory in the hills of Wales:
Caverns of light revealed the Holy Grail
Exhaling gold upon the mountain-tops;
At "Holy! Holy! Holy!" in the Mass
King Brychan's sainted children crowded round,
And past and present were enwrapped in one.

In quest of mystical experience
I knelt in darkness at St. Enodoc;
I visited our local Holy Well,
Whereto the native Cornish still resort
For cures for whooping-cough, and drop bent pins
Into its peaty water . . . Not a sign:
No mystical experience was vouchsafed:
The maidenhair just trembled in the wind

And everything looked as it always looked . . .
But somewhere, somewhere underneath the dunes,
Somewhere among the cairns or in the caves
The Celtic saints would come to me, the ledge
Of time we walk on, like a thin cliff-path
High in the mist, would show the precipice.

*　　*　　*

DISTANT VIEW OF A PROVINCIAL TOWN

Beside those spires so spick and span
    Against an unencumbered sky
The old Great Western Railway ran
    When someone different was I.

St. Aidan's with the prickly knobs
    And iron spikes and coloured tiles—
Where Auntie Maud devoutly bobs
    In those enriched vermilion aisles:

St. George's where the mattins bell
    But rarely drowned the trams for prayer—
No Popish sight or sound or smell
    Disturbed that gas-invaded air:

St. Mary's where the Rector preached
    In such a jolly friendly way
On cricket, football, things that reached
    The simple life of every day:

And that United Benefice
    With entrance permanently locked,
How Gothic, grey and sad it is
    Since Mr. Grogley was unfrocked!

The old Great Western Railway shakes
    The old Great Western Railway spins—
The old Great Western Railway makes
    Me very sorry for my sins.

CHRISTMAS

The bells of waiting Advent ring,
　　The Tortoise stove is lit again
And lamp-oil light across the night
　　Has caught the streaks of winter rain
In many a stained-glass window sheen
From Crimson Lake to Hooker's Green.

The holly in the windy hedge
　　And round the Manor House the yew
Will soon be stripped to deck the ledge,
　　The altar, font and arch and pew,
So that the villagers can say
"The church looks nice" on Christmas Day.

Provincial public houses blaze
　　And Corporation tramcars clang,
On lighted tenements I gaze
　　Where paper decorations hang,
And bunting in the red Town Hall
Says "Merry Christmas to you all."

And London shops on Christmas Eve
　　Are strung with silver bells and flowers
As hurrying clerks the City leave
　　To pigeon-haunted classic towers,
And marbled clouds go scudding by
The many-steepled London sky.

And girls in slacks remember Dad,
　　And oafish louts remember Mum,
And sleepless children's hearts are glad,
　　And Christmas-morning bells say "Come!"
Even to shining ones who dwell
Safe in the Dorchester Hotel.

And is it true? And is it true,
    This most tremendous tale of all,
Seen in a stained-glass window's hue,
    A Baby in an ox's stall?
The Maker of the stars and sea
Become a Child on earth for me?

And is it true? For if it is,
    No loving fingers tying strings
Around those tissued fripperies,
    The sweet and silly Christmas things
Bath salts and inexpensive scent
And hideous tie so kindly meant.

No love that in a family dwells,
    No carolling in frosty air,
Nor all the steeple-shaking bells
    Can with this single Truth compare—
That God was Man in Palestine
And lives to-day in Bread and Wine.

NOTES

1. POEMS OF CHILDHOOD

p. 9.   SUMMONED BY BELLS

John Betjeman lived, as a child, in a house on Highgate West Hill. This is a steep hill that runs down from the village of Highgate—to the north of central London—to Parliament Hill Fields, then on to Kentish Town. To the left of this long, curving hill, as you go up it, lies Hampstead Heath and miles of woodland of the Kenwood estate. The Betjemans' house was also on the left of the hill, with its back to the Heath. Millfield and Merton Lanes run off the main road on to the Heath, Merton above the Betjemans' house, and Millfield below it.

hornbeams: trees of hard, tough wood, like beeches.

Middlesex: at that time Highgate was in the county of Middlesex.

Delaunay-Belleville: one of the first makes of motor-car.

Constable: John Constable (1776–1837) was one of the greatest realistic landscape painters of the nineteenth-century English countryside.

Keats: the poet John Keats (1795–1821) lived in Hampstead for some years—on the other side of the Heath from Highgate. The street where he lived is now called Keats' Grove.

Caenwood Towers: a beautiful house with a most impressive central tower built in 1870 on the edge of the Kenwood estate.

Grand Duke Michael's house: a house that John glimpsed behind a tree-shaded drive, near Caenwood Towers.

Holly Lodge: a house built high on the eastern side of Highgate West Hill that was the home of the Baroness Burdett-Coutts (1814–1906), a wealthy, generous woman, noted for her works of charity.

p. 9. John Betjeman's father worked in the family business in Islington. The firm made period furniture, silverware and all kinds of bric-à-brac, so the family was comfortably well off, but not wealthy. In those days—round about 1912—people were very conscious of social differences. The working classes, the middle classes, the upper classes and the aristocracy were all sharply divided from each other, and there were all kinds of sub-divisions within each class. Everyone was able to feel superior to someone else, but inferior to others. It was only in the working classes that things were different. There a unity of spirit and comradeship existed between the poor people who were all struggling against the same thing—want. John's father, a 'middle-class' businessman, living by trade, would be considered lower in status than someone from the upper classes whose money probably came from land, property or industry, or from a family fortune he had inherited.

John Betjeman soon became aware of these class differences as a small boy. He knew that financially his family were higher than the people next door, but lower than those in the grander houses up the hill, whose owners kept carriages and hosts of servants. This awareness of class differences stayed with him all his life and he grew up to be amused by the false and artificial barriers that people put up between each other, based only on income or family origins.

When John was told that the name Betjeman was German he was very upset. There was a good deal of anti-German feeling in Britain before the outbreak of the 1914–1918 war, and anything that could be accused of being German, however wrongly, was liable to be insulted or abused. The tide of national, patriotic feeling was at its height, and to be 'pure British' was the only way of being above reproach.

The name Betjeman was not German anyway; it was Dutch, but the neighbour's comments were enough to set John's mind wondering whether he was as safe and secure as he thought he was. Perhaps there was something strange about his family that made them outcasts and different from other people?

> *Burdett-Coutts estate:* the grounds of Holly Lodge extended to the foot of the hill and formed the view from the front of the Betjemans' house. Now this parkland has become a huge, ugly housing estate.
>
> *brougham:* a one-horsed, closed carriage.

p. 10. Although the seeds of a wrong and destructive idea had been sown in the little boy's mind, he loved his home and the beauties of the Highgate landscape about him, and, above all, Archibald, his toy bear.

> *nonconformist Chetwynd Road:* one of the turnings off the main road with a Baptist chapel on the corner.
>
> *Kentish Town:* a poor district of London at the end of Highgate Road, the road that Highgate West Hill becomes as it continues downwards.
>
> *Selfridge's:* one of the biggest department stores in London.
>
> *Bon Marché:* the name of a draper's shop with many branches where things were cheap and good.
>
> *Electric Palace:* an early cinema that showed silent films.
>
> *eyrie:* a bird's nest built high up, like that of an eagle. In this sense it is the Betjeman house, high up on the hill.
>
> *North London:* the railway which ran across north London from Broad Street in the City, westwards to Richmond in Surrey.
>
> *Gospel Oak:* a station near Kentish Town, on the North London Railway.

p. 10. Mrs. Betjeman, like many ladies of her day, would entertain visitors and have her 'at homes'. Every second Thursday of the month a number of her friends would arrive to play Auction Bridge. They took the game very seriously and often became quite heated, hurling acid remarks at one another. It was the custom then for small children to have to call 'Aunt' any female friend, as well as relative, of the family.

Votes for Women: this was a slogan much in use from about 1908 onwards when women began campaigning to be allowed a vote in the election of Members of Parliament. This was finally granted to them in 1928 after a long and hard struggle.

London Pride: a small, pink flower to be found in many town gardens.

p. 12.   GROUP LIFE: LETCHWORTH

Another kind of childhood. In this poem a modern, over-enthusiastic mother is talking the kind of nonsense about her children that is so often exchanged over the garden fence, or outside the local super-market. She seems to have given some of her children exotic and wildly unsuitable names, too, like 'Aluréd' and 'Sympathy'.

weal: welfare.

Morris Dancers: Morris Dancing is a kind of English country dancing, dating from medieval times, for which traditional dress is worn.

ex-Service man: demobilized from the army, and probably wounded in the war. In this poem he is the lodger of the woman who is speaking.

kinderbank: a sand pit where children can play.

p. 13.   FALSE SECURITY

This is an incident from John Betjeman's childhood in Highgate that shows again how people could be pre-occupied with social differences, even at the risk of deeply hurting a small child's feelings. John braves the winter darkness of West Hill, with its trees and hedges and imaginary ghosts, and struggles to the top. He is going to a party. When he gets there he feels the house to be warm and friendly, and the party wonderful. So is the little hostess who holds his hand. Then comes the horrible blow. When the guests are leaving he hears the mother tell one of them he is a 'common little boy'. His whole illusion is shattered and all his feelings of success and security wither at this awful accusation of social inferiority.

The Grove: a row of big houses at the top of the hill in Highgate Village.

Daniel Neal: a London shop specializing in children's wear, particularly shoes.

Heal: a London store, known for its furnishings and good quality materials.

p. 14.   CROYDON

This is about the childhood of a boy of the 1870's—'Uncle Dick'—who was born in Croydon when it was a growing Victorian town of Surrey, surrounded by woodland, fields and unspoiled country.

Whitgift: the famous public school at Croydon.

spadgers: the cockney word for sparrows.

p. 14.   INDOOR GAMES NEAR NEWBURY

Here is another children's party. The ending this time is happy, for Wendy,
the hostess, has chosen the little boy as her special friend; and when he is
taken home and put to bed, he is full of dreams and happiness about her.

Lagonda, Hupmobile, Delage: makes of motor-car.

Victrola: an early make of gramophone.

featly: nimbly.

2. DISCOVERING POETRY

p. 19.   SUMMONED BY BELLS

The urge to write poetry came to John Betjeman when he was seven years old.
He was bursting with ideas for things he wanted to write about, but had no
ability to express them on paper. Two of the places he most wanted to write
about were Highgate and the near-by heathland where he lived, and the sea
coast near Trebetherick in north Cornwall where he spent his summer holidays.
But however hard he tried, no inspiration came, and the verses he wrote filled
him with shame when he was a little older. Yet he went on trying, whatever
the discouragements. The two poems that follow in this section are what
Betjeman wrote many years later on the two subjects that had meant so much to
him as a child.

Cambridge comes a wind: John Betjeman's University was Oxford, and,
     because of the traditional rivalry between the two universities, he still
     feels the cold wind of criticism coming from Cambridge to disparage
     his achievements.

internal rhyming: the 'internal rhymes' of Shelley's 'Cloud' can be seen
     in the first and third lines:

> I bring fresh showers for the thirsting flowers,
>   From the seas and the streams;
> I bear light shade for the leaves when laid
>   In their noonday dreams.

Polzeath Bay: in north Cornwall, near Trebetherick.

St. Michael's church: on top of the hill in Highgate village. Its spire can
     be seen from many points of the heath.

parodies of A & M: Betjeman felt his poems to be feeble and rather
     ridiculous versions of *Hymns Ancient and Modern.*

Haslemere: a town in Surrey.

Allingham: William Allingham (1824–1889) was author of the famous
     poem 'The Fairies':

> Up the airy mountain,
>   Down the rushy glen,
> We daren't go a-hunting
>   For fear of little men . . .

rhymes A B, A B: the form of verse in which the first and third lines rhyme, so do the second and fourth.

thin St. Anne's: the church at the bottom of Highgate West Hill.

Fitzroy Park: the old carriage road from Highgate village to Fitzroy House. The Fitzroy estate is very near to that of Kenwood.

Holly Village: the cluster of spiky, gabled Victorian houses beside the Holly Lodge estate, near Highgate Cemetery.

Frank Bramley: (1857–1905) a late-Victorian painter whose famous picture 'The Hopeless Dawn' still hangs in the Tate Gallery in London.

Greenaway: a beach between Trebetherick and Polzeath Bay in north Cornwall.

p. 22.   GREENAWAY

The poem describes the beach at Greenaway, washed by powerful and dangerous seas. John Betjeman knows it well and feels safe on its familiar stretch of shingle. Yet in a dream he has seen it from the sea, and has felt the unseen terrors beneath its beauty.

bladder-wrack: a common seaweed with bubble-like swellings in its fronds.

cowrie: a kind of sea-shell.

p. 23.   PARLIAMENT HILL FIELDS

As Highgate West Hill becomes Highgate Road, and continues past Parliament Hill Fields down to Kentish Town, the district becomes dingy with factories, breweries, laundries and coal merchants' yards. In Betjeman's boyhood, horse-trams ran up and down this road and under the railway bridge of the old Great Eastern branch line to Gospel Oak. A journey back to Highgate West Hill from a shopping expedition in Kentish Town was like a journey into a different world; the one, industrial, poor and gloomy; and the other, light, airy and green.

Midland: the Midland Railway that used to run from St. Pancras to the North.

Cricklewood: a district in north-west London served by the Midland Railway, later the 'London, Midland and Scottish'.

Charrington, Sells, Dale and Co.: a firm of coal merchants with an office outside Kentish Town station. Their offices were often seen on London railway approach roads.

bobble-hanging plane: the fruit of the plane-tree that hangs down in little bobbles.

ashlar-speckled: uneven colouring of masonry made of large blocks of stone, smooth-faced and square-edged.

Eighteen-sixty Early English: Early English was the style of Gothic architecture that flourished between about 1180 and 1270. In the nineteenth century, churches were again built in the Gothic styles and this was called the 'Gothic Revival'.

3. POEMS OF EARLY SCHOOL

p. 27.   SUMMONED BY BELLS

Peggy Purey-Cust was John Betjeman's first love. Peggy's golden hair and blue eyes made going to school a joy for him. He saw her as the heroine of all his favourite stories and once went to tea at her house. But he was never invited again and Peggy was always 'out' when he called. In fact she disappeared from the scene altogether, and going to school became a miserable business, especially when two bullies of boys beset his route. And, what was worse, the bullies changed schools when he did and they all went to Highgate Junior School together. He dreaded going back after holidays.

Byron House: an infant school in The Grove, Highgate Village.

blob-work: a kind of painting that was taught to small children.

spired St. Pancras: there is a splendid view across London from Highgate Village, and it would have been easy to see the spires of St. Pancras Station and the dome of St. Paul's Cathedral from Peggy's drawing-room.

Walter Crane: (1845–1915) an artist, illustrator and designer who, like William Morris, set a new fashion for interior decoration towards the end of the nineteenth century.

harbinger: one who goes ahead to announce the arrival of something or somebody.

Avernus: a hell-hole. Avernus is a lake in Campania, Italy, formed in an old volcanic crater with no natural outlet. It appears frequently in Greek and Roman history and was believed once to have been the entrance by which the Greek heroes Odysseus and Æneas descended into the infernal regions.

H. M. Brock: (1875–1960), an illustrator of books, especially school stories.

p. 28.   AN INCIDENT IN THE EARLY LIFE OF EBENEZER JONES, POET,
1828

This poem is about another boy who went to school at Highgate, almost one hundred years before John Betjeman. He was Ebenezer Jones, who, after an unhappy boyhood in a strict, Methodist family, became a clerk in a city firm, working twelve hours daily. The dishonest practices that went on there upset him very much, and he managed to get away and become an accountant. He wanted to write poetry, and did write as much as time and rather poor health allowed him. A disastrous marriage and the poor reception by the critics of his book of poems, *Studies of Sensation and Event,* sent his health into further decline, but at the end of his life Dante Gabriel Rossetti revived public interest in his work, and people began to realize that Ebenezer Jones was, for all his unevenness, a poet of power and genius. *Studies of Sensation and Event* was re-issued, with the help of Ebenezer's brother Sumner, and Ebenezer wrote some new poems which show him at the height of his powers. Before he died he was acclaimed as a very considerable poet by many of his contemporaries. Today he is not widely known, but the best of his poems are still said by critics to rank among the finest of their kind in English literature.

School in Ebenezer's day was often harsh and brutal, and this incident of cruelty to a dog shows the kind of thing that could easily happen when a vicious, bullying master was out to keep his pupils in fear of him.

(Introduction)

dissenting minister: nonconformist clergyman, in this instance, a Calvinistic Methodist.

conning our tasks: learning our lessons.

lurcher dog: the lurcher is a cross-breed between a collie or sheep-dog and a greyhound.

choleric: bad-tempered.

usher: assistant schoolmaster.

(Poem)

dray: a heavy, horse-drawn cart.

stucco: plaster used for coating wall surfaces and for the moulding of architectural decorations.

Holloway: district to the south of Highgate.

Dissenting chapels: nonconformist chapels.

Grecian squares: many of the squares in that part of London are designed on spacious, classical lines, including Canonbury Square, where Ebenezer Jones was born.

Saints: in this sense 'Saints' are people who belong to one of the nonconformist religious sects. These sects were formed by people who had broken away from the Established Church, and then broken away from each other ('Seceders from the Protestant Secessions'). At the beginning of the nineteenth century many of these people were becoming wealthy through trade and industry, and this continued as the century went on.

godly usher: many of the people who professed a strict religious observance, and practised church-going with fanatical zeal, behaved in a very un-Christian way in their daily lives. So the 'godly usher' would have no twinges of conscience when punishing his class of terror-stricken little boys, or throwing a dog to its death down the stairs. He would feel that he was establishing law and order in the name of God, in fact he says so quite plainly: 'I am his word.'

Calvin's God: Calvin (1509–1564) was the great Swiss divine and reformer who developed the doctrines of earlier reformers and preached that man is born in sin through Adam's fall. He said that man, therefore, is depraved, corrupt and hateful to God, and his only hope of redemption is by faith in God, repentance and strict mortification of the flesh. Calvin also believed in 'election', which is the doctrine that some are predestined to damnation by God and others predestined to salvation. The 'godly usher' smugly thought he was 'saved' and could therefore do no wrong.

4. POEMS OF HOLIDAYS

p. 33.   SUMMONED BY BELLS

Most of John Betjeman's early holidays were spent in north Cornwall. As a small boy, hygienically cared for and nourished with all the patent foods that were good for children, he would be taken on the familiar journey to Cornwall, travelling by the express train that left from Waterloo. Then would follow the drive to the village of Trebetherick in a horse-drawn carriage, and John would be excited and curious about all the people and things he remembered from times before.

On his first morning he would rush off to the beach before breakfast, and then would follow long days of bathing, climbing, visits to the farm and all the joys of the sea and country.

John Betjeman begins this section of *Summoned by Bells* in the style adopted by the great Greek poets at the beginning of one of their epics, or stories in blank verse. The Greeks would always begin by calling upon one of their gods for inspiration, and after invoking the god in grand and magnificent language, they would call upon some of the kindred gods as well. After that, the story proper would begin.

> Lines 2–6 list some of the much advertised patent foods, tonics, soap and toothpaste that were said to be best for health and hygiene.
>
> *Free Thought, Fresh Air:* in this sense, gods kindred to hygiene in the realms of health and well-being.
>
> *Egloskerry, Tresméer:* two villages in Cornwall on the main railway line.
>
> *Bible Christians:* the Bible Christians formed an offshoot of Methodism that was peculiar to Cornwall. They were simple people who held revival meetings and founded chapels of their own. They were not at all like Calvinists; they were much more like the Salvation Army.
>
> *Wadebridge:* the small port and railway-town on the river Camel which is the nearest point to the coastal villages near Polzeath in north Cornwall.
>
> *Trebetherick:* a village near Polzeath.
>
> *neap:* point at which high tides, at first and third quarters of the moon, are at their lowest.
>
> *Doom Bar:* a dangerous, sandy part of the estuary on which ships had often been wrecked.
>
> *pennywort:* a plant with round, cup-shaped leaves that often grows in crevices of rocks and walls.
>
> *fennel:* a wild herb.

lugworm: worms found in sand of the sea shore, used as bait for fishing.
oyster-catcher: a black-backed bird, about the size of the common gull,
that lives in rocky, sandy shores, particularly on the west coast. It has
a long, bright orange bill and eats small fish, shrimps and shell-fish.
sandhoppers: tiny, shell-covered animals that live on the sea shore.
elvers: baby eels.
tamarisks: feathery, evergreen shrubs with pink or white flowers.
convolvulus: a twining plant with a bell-like flower.
sea-pink: a common sea plant also called 'thrift'. It has a tough, strong
root.

p. 35. SEASIDE GOLF
Golf links beside the sea can often fill the player with more zest and well-being
than those inland, for there is the view, the sound of the sea and the smell of it.
The only games John Betjeman really enjoys are golf and tennis, and this poem
tells of the time when he was so inspired by sea breezes over a game of golf
that he got his ball into the hole in only three strokes. Never had he done it
before!

p. 36. TREBETHERICK
This poem describes Trebetherick in sunny, calm weather and in a storm.
It ends with a prayer that the wonderful days of happiness the little boy John
and his friends had there may be given in time to their children too.
    lichen: a green, fungus-like moss that grows on trees and rocks.
    Shilla Mill: a water mill up a wooded valley behind Polzeath.
    St. Enodoc: an early Welsh saint of the Celtic Church which flourished
    in Cornwall in the sixth and seventh centuries. The little thirteenth-
    century church close by the sea was named after him. The church was
    once partially buried under the sand dunes, but was dug out again
    during the nineteenth century.

p. 37. EAST ANGLIAN BATHE
This is about another of John Betjeman's holidays, this time in Norfolk. Horsey
Mere is a lake—one of the Norfolk 'Broads'—a little inland from the sea shore.
The East Anglian coast is often very cold for bathing, especially in windy
weather.
    leeside: the sheltered side, away from the wind.
    adumbration: casting shadows.

p. 38. BESIDE THE SEASIDE
A poem about a different kind of holiday—the organized family holiday that
many people have when they go for their yearly fortnight to a 'popular
resort'. Often they stay in a boarding house or have 'bed and breakfast' in a
house where rooms are let. The wealthier people stay in hotels. Yet for all these
people their particular piece of seaside—'Sandy Cove' in this poem—means

everything. They have been going there for years and probably wouldn't think of going anywhere else. Its pleasures are known and familiar, and however expensive and over-crowded it becomes, hundreds of families will come flocking back every year.

The story of Jennifer and Mr. Pedder is sad but only too likely. Perhaps Jennifer took it too much to heart, for all through life people have wonderful moments of success and favouritism, and other less happy moments of failure when nobody seems to want them.

But while Jennifer's heart is breaking and the grown-ups worry about class differences—are they better or worse, richer or poorer than their fellow holiday-makers?—the sea, powerful and timeless, goes on washing the shore as it has for thousands of years.

Green Shutters, Windyridge, High Dormers: typical names of family houses in town and suburb.

quartz: rough, shiny stone that is often embedded on the tops of garden walls.

macrocarpa: a kind of cypress tree.

Esplanade: the promenade—the road along the sea front which usually contains shops and amusement arcades.

hydrangea: a well-known shrub with pink, blue or white flowers, often grown in tubs outside houses or on terraces.

escallonia: a shrub with a pink flower and shiny leaf.

lodging-house: seaside lodging-houses can often be uncomfortable and very dreary. In this one—typical of many—visitors have to keep to the landlady's rules and are expected to be out all day. The visitors' lounge is small enough and ugly enough to deter anyone from wanting to go into it, however hard it might be raining outside!

secretarial work: this reference to Jennifer's work with the Board of Trade in later life means that she didn't marry and have children of her own. She was so upset by Mr. Pedder's snub to her that she never got over it, and was suspicious of all young men from then on.

lissomest: the most supple and agile of all.

début: first appearance.

interstices: crevices or chinks in the rocks.

Humoresque: Dvořák's famous *Humoresque*, which is often played by bands in special arrangements for brass instruments—or 'silver bands' whose brass instruments appear to be made of silver.

Rudge: a make of bicycle.

Flannel Dance: a dance where people went in informal clothes such as flannel trousers and blazers.

the strange starfish: John Betjeman finds the starfish a most alarming creature because, unlike other living creatures he knows, it is so impersonal that it is almost one with the rocks on which it rests. It is mysterious and unaccountable.

p. 44.   HUNTER TRIALS
A nonsense-poem about pony-loving girls who like to spend as much of their
holidays as they can on horseback.

5. POEMS OF PEOPLE

p. 49.   SUMMONED BY BELLS
Some of the best known of John Betjeman's poems are his verse portraits of
people. From childhood he has always had heroes and heroines to look up to,
and it is them he describes with such candour and shrewdness: the school
prefect who was the kind of ideal boy that Betjeman felt he ought to be, but
never could be; and, in later life, the strong, brawny sports girls who made
him fall in love with them for their skill and vitality. (He always hated sports
at school himself and was no good at games.)
   The 'Percival Mandeville' extract from *Summoned by Bells* comes from the
beginning of the chapter about going to private boarding school. The lie
Betjeman told to get out of fighting reflects with great credit on Mandeville,
who, strong and clever though he was, would never 'hit a chap when he was
down'.
      North and Hillard: a Latin text-book.

p. 50.   THE OLYMPIC GIRL
Here is the kind of athletic, Amazon girl that makes Betjeman feel small and
weak by comparison. He feels very unworthy of her, but wishes he were her
tennis-racket, for then, at least, she would take some notice of him.
      retroussé : turned up.
      εἴθε γενοίμην : 'would I were'.
      Rupert Brooke: (1887-1915). This refers to a quotation from Brooke's
      poem 'The Old Vicarage, Grantchester'. Grantchester is a village
      outside Cambridge, Brooke's university town.
               εἴθε γενοίμην ... would I were
               In Grantchester, in Grantchester!

p. 51.   HOW TO GET ON IN SOCIETY
A light-hearted verse portrait of a lady who is trying hard to acquire the kind
of etiquette she believes will place her firmly in the 'upper classes' in the eyes
of her friends and neighbours. In the 1920's and after, words like 'serviettes',
'toilet', 'lounge', 'doileys' became passwords of middle-class respectability.

p. 52.   POT POURRI FROM A SURREY GARDEN
The rhythm of this poem is strong and free, unlike the more formal rhythms
used in most of the other poems. Each line goes with a swing that depends for
its pace and effect on the skilful use of words. This is the kind of poem that

should be read and enjoyed for the atmosphere and meaning *suggested* by the words, rather than for the literal meaning of each word in turn.

Pam is another muscular, tennis-playing sports girl who lives in Surrey. Surrey is not quite country, not quite London; it is something in between. When the railway came to it at the end of the nineteenth century, it made it possible for people to travel from there each day to their work in London. John Betjeman sees Surrey as an uncountrified, littered county, with Victorian churches built in the developed areas, and well-appointed villas belonging to prosperous businessmen, dotted among the conifer trees.

> *Pot Pourri :* a mixture or selection. There was a famous late Victorian book called *Pot Pourri from a Surrey Garden* by Mrs. C. W. Earle. It was written as a diary of everyday events and was dedicated to her sister Lady Constance Lytton. Apart from Mrs. Earle's reflections on life in general the book gave valuable advice on gardening and cooking as well as all kinds of household hints.

Weights: a brand of cigarette.

Malvernian: Malvern is a well-known public school in Worcestershire.

Woking: a Surrey town.

Hendren: a famous cricketer.

Gothic enlacement: Victorian Gothic arches cutting into one another.

Licensed: married.

p. 53.   IN THE PUBLIC GARDENS
Another light-hearted poem about two English people having a gay time in Vienna. The simplicity of the rhythm and the delightful use of the words *Eingang* and *Ausgang* conjure up the whole Viennese mood of the poem and make it easy to remember.

> *Strauss:* Johann Strauss (1825–1899), the famous composer of waltzes.
>
> *Eingang:* way in.
>
> *Ausgang:* way out.
>
> *electroliers:* clusters of electric lamps like chandeliers.
>
> *Zwei Engländer:* two English people.

p. 53.   A SUBALTERN'S LOVE-SONG
Joan Hunter Dunn is perhaps the most famous of all Betjeman's heroines. Again the setting is Surrey with its villas and conifers, its prosperous middle-class families, their sports clubs and cars. This time it is a Subaltern, a junior officer training at Aldershot, the near-by Army centre, who sings his song of praise. He is in love with the beautiful tennis-girl, and by the end of the poem he has got himself engaged to her, so his rhapsody is not in vain.

> *euonymus:* a kind of shrub.
>
> '*not adopted*': these are roads that are the responsibility of the house-owners in them, not of the local council. Often they are unmade and little more than well-worn mud tracks.

Camberley: the Surrey town which contains the famous officers' training academy of Sandhurst.

ominous: foreshadowing disaster. The Subaltern was obviously not a good dancer and was afraid of what Miss Hunter Dunn would think of his clumsiness.

p. 55.   THE OLD LIBERALS

A sympathetic portrait of two rather faded people who, in a previous generation, would have stood for all that was progressive in intellectual thinking and the arts. The scene is Boar's Hill, an early suburb of Oxford. These were the people who had reflected the influence of William Morris (1834–1896), an artist and thinker who was one of the great figures of his age. Morris was also a craftsman; he designed furniture, textiles and anything connected with interior decoration. He was a poet and, towards the end of his life, he became an active pioneer for Socialism. His followers, like this elderly gentleman and his daughter, led simple, creative lives, filling their homes with artistic things and believing that human beings would all be happier if they would do the same and resist the coming of the mechanized age with its threat of destruction to individual thinking. Now, after the passing of years, they make music together and look sadly at the ugliness and vulgarity of modern life around them and see how far it has drifted from the ideals in which they believed.

Pale green: green is the Liberal colour.

Yattendon hymns: The Yattendon Hymnal was compiled at the end of the nineteenth century by Robert Bridges and H. Ellis Wooldridge. Some of the hymns were translated from Latin and Greek for the first time. The book was famous in its day and many of the hymns have passed into common usage. The hymnal is still in use now at Yattendon in Berkshire, where Robert Bridges lived.

hautbois: the old way of spelling 'oboe', the woodwind instrument.

William de Morgan: (1839–1917). An artist and novelist, famous for the beautiful tiles he made to decorate the interiors of houses.

wains: waggons.

swains: country lads.

ted: spread out for drying.

p. 56.   LORD COZENS HARDY

This is a poem about the ghost of the first Lord Cozens Hardy seen by Norfolk villagers at a certain time of the year. The village is Letheringsett, near Holt, in north Norfolk, where the present Lord Cozens Hardy still owns Letheringsett Hall. But the poem is not based on truth. There is no mausoleum, no ghost, and the legend is imaginary, inspired by John Betjeman's visit to the village, and the idea it gave him for a good story.

Doric: style of architecture based on the Greek. This portico would have large, Doric pillars.

All Souls: The feast of All Saints, or All Souls, on the first of November every year.

Master of the Rolls: a judge in the Court of Appeal who is also in charge of certain public records.

p. 57. EXCHANGE OF LIVINGS

The chief delight of this poem is its play on the word 'incumbent', an ungainly and rather comic word when repeated often enough within a few sentences. It means 'the holder of office', and here the office is that of vicar of the parish. One clergyman has answered the advertisement of another who wants to move to a different parish. The two clergymen meet and compare notes on their respective parishes to decide whether they will make a swap.

supine: lying down—probably lazing in a deck-chair with his feet up.

A and M: Hymns Ancient and Modern.

recumbent: lying down.

Rector . . . Cripplegate: he would be the kind of vicar that lived miles away from his parish and visited it on Sundays to take the statutory services. City of London churches have very few resident parishioners anyway. (See p. 123; note on *Summoned by Bells*, Poems of Places.)

p. 58. DIARY OF A CHURCH MOUSE

The church mouse is one of the most charming and lovable of all John Betjeman's characters. She has a simple but shrewd outlook on life, living humbly in a forgotten junk cupboard, and getting little to eat except once a year at Harvest Festival. But how unfair it is, she thinks, that rats and mice from all around, who are never seen near the church the rest of the year, should come at Harvest Festival and greedily eat the food they have no right to. Some, she knows, have no religion at all, and some are of quite different religions, yet that does not stop them coming to steal the Church of England's festival food.

The little mouse is quite sure that human beings wouldn't behave so badly. Yet on second thoughts, perhaps she's wrong? For who are all those people who fill the church on Harvest Festival Sunday whom she's never seen before? Are humans as bad as the animals and come to church only on the big festivals, but not on all the other Sundays of the year?

pagan: heathen.

papistical: following the Church of Rome.

6. DISCOVERING ARCHITECTURE

p. 63. SUMMONED BY BELLS

It was while he was at private boarding school—the Dragon School in Oxford—that John Betjeman began to take an interest in church architecture. He found a book that contained Victorian water-colour pictures of buildings, and that set him off on his bicycle in search of village churches. One of the masters at the school helped and encouraged him, and his enthusiasm grew as he learned more and more from what he observed.

The lyric poem about the school picnic and orchid hunt follows straight on and ends the chapter of *Summoned by Bells* that is about John Betjeman's private school days.

Chaundy's shop: a bookshop in Oxford that used to be in the Broad, but was pulled down when the New Bodleian Library was built on its site.

ilex tree: the evergreen oak tree that grows in Worcester College Gardens.

Magdalen: Magdalen College, Oxford, the college to which Betjeman went as an undergraduate later on.

The High: the main street in Oxford where many colleges stand. Said at one time to be one of the most beautiful streets in Europe.

Univ.: University College, Oxford.

Norm.: Norman architecture, dating from 1066 to about 1180.

E.E.: Early English, the first great style of Gothic architecture, from about 1180 to 1270.

Dec.: Decorated, the second style of Gothic architecture, from about 1270 to 1380.

Perp.: Perpendicular, the third style of Gothic architecture from 1380 to the Reformation in the sixteenth century.

vaulting shafts . . . groins: these are all architectural terms for parts of church construction.

Harrow and Keble: Gerald Haynes went to public school at Harrow and to university at Keble College, Oxford.

tympana . . . Norfolk screens: more architectural terms for parts of church construction.

bindweed: convolvulus, a climbing wild plant.

Red Sea troops: Moses led the children of Israel across the Red Sea to escape the Egyptian pursuers. The Lord caused the water to be divided so that it stood still, like a wall on either side of them, and they walked across on a path of dry land. (Exodus 14.)

Sturmey-Archer: the three-speed gear of the bicycle.

p. 66.   HYMN

A fashion existed in the second half of the nineteenth century for 'restoring', or re-designing, ancient churches and building new ones in the medieval 'Gothic' style. The work was often paid for by wealthy industrialists and landowners. The rectors of the old churches invariably welcomed the new 'improvements'—this one did, particularly as some of the old carved wood-work was transferred to his own hall. This poem describes the changes that were made to many churches at the time. The 'he' is, of course, the architect who was responsible for it all.

encaustic tile: tile inlaid with coloured clays which are burnt in.

p. 67.   AN ARCHÆOLOGICAL PICNIC

The poet and his friend Mary have packed their picnic lunch and bottles of lemonade and gone off in search of antiquities. They have their picnic in a field, then go into the village church, but Mary soon sees enough of the church and the boy sends her back to the field to drink more lemonade while he stays to examine the church's architecture more closely.

> *Blunden time:* the poet Edmund Blunden (born 1896) was one of the poets who wrote about the First World War, having fought in it himself. Blunden is also known as a very fine pastoral poet. Particularly beautiful are the poems where he is describing his native Kent. So 'Blunden time' means a time of country quiet.
>
> *Lady's Finger, Smokewort, Lovers' Loss:* wild plants that grow in fields and hedgerows.
>
> *Tennysonian chime:* 'The mellow lin-lan-lone of evening bells' is a phrase Tennyson uses in the poem 'Far-Far-Away' to describe three bells ringing in a country church.
>
> *where the key lies . . . .:* the church porch where, in the Middle Ages all the business of the village was conducted. That is why public notices are always hung there to this day.
>
> *cerements:* grave clothes.
>
> *Burne-Jones:* Sir Edward Burne-Jones (1833–1898) was one of the great 'Pre-Raphaelite' artists of the nineteenth century who designed and made some of the loveliest of stained-glass windows in English churches.
>
> *Trans arcade:* arches built in the Transitional style. This style came between the rounded arches of the Norman and the pointed arches of the Gothic.
>
> *squinch and squint:* architectural terms for parts of church construction.

p. 67.   SUNDAY MORNING, KING'S CAMBRIDGE

The chapel of King's College, Cambridge, is one of the most beautiful buildings in the country and is a major achievement of English medieval architecture. It was built between 1448 and 1515 in Perpendicular style. The choir of this chapel is equally famous, and every Christmas Eve it sings the Festival of Nine Lessons and Carols which is now always broadcast. This poem describes some of the interior of the chapel and Betjeman's reflections as the choir files in to begin morning service.

> *plaster Gothic:* examples of early Victorian Gothic Revival plasterwork that can be seen on some of the Cambridge college buildings, e.g., Sidney Sussex College.

p. 68.   THE TOWN CLERK'S VIEWS

Quite a different attitude to architecture is expressed here. John Betjeman feels that one of the disasters of the present age is the passion for pulling down relics of past beauties and achievements, and replacing them with ugly, shoddy, stream-lined things designed for utility. This is a rather bitter verse-portrait of the kind of official who holds the views Betjeman most dislikes, and is, unhappily, in a position to put them into operation. He is the kind of power-seeking little man who is responsible for turning 'our country into hell'.

hipp'd roof: roof with two different angles on one slope.

aquatint: a picture printed by a special process of engraving on copper. Particularly popular in the nineteenth century.

Branksome Chine: a valley in Bournemouth leading to the sea.

Torquay: this was a fashionable health and holiday resort in Devonshire much favoured by the wealthy in Victorian times.

Oxford: the industrial development in and around Oxford in recent years has caused distress to all who love and respect the town with its ancient colleges and beautiful buildings. This has not yet happened to Cambridge.

Welwyn: Welwyn Garden City in Hertfordshire was one of the first 'Garden Cities' built at the beginning of this century. It was a planned attempt to build a town which preserved the feel and appearance of the countryside.

Middle West: The Middle West is one great region in the U.S.A. with Chicago at its centre. John Betjeman is thinking of the unimaginative mass-produced architecture which has been fostered by swift industrial expansion.

Broadway: in Gloucestershire. This is already a Cotswold show village, visited by thousands of tourists every year.

Eurythmic: the practice of bodily movement to music.

7. POEMS OF PLACES

p. 75.   SUMMONED BY BELLS

Places have always been important to John Betjeman. This extract from *Summoned by Bells* tells what a wrench it was for him when his parents moved from Highgate to Chelsea. Their whole outlook on life seemed to change with the move—now they were prosperous and mixing with artistic, advanced-thinking people of a higher social standing, and John hated being uprooted. He missed the old haunts and couldn't get used to the new house. So he spent as much time away from it as possible, touring the London Underground with a friend, and visiting churches and old buildings. On Sundays his favourite churches were in the City where hardly a soul would be in attendance but the statutory services had to take place all the same.

In all Betjeman's poems, there is a great sense of 'place'. Whether he is writing about Miss Joan Hunter Dunn or Ebenezer Jones, the background is not merely indicated by a few general impressions; it is described in detail, with familiar objects, smells and noises. It is not surprising that in this section, 'Poems of Places', there are more poems than in any other of the book, for there is a very large number to choose from.

> *Augustus John:* (1878–1961). A famous artist who lived in Chelsea for many years and was considered to live the model 'bohemian', free-thinking life. Art students liked to copy him, and wealthy or otherwise distinguished people liked to know him—or, better still, have their portraits painted by him.
>
> *divorce:* in the 1920's it was considered very daring to bring into the open a subject which had hitherto been suppressed in all genteel society.
>
> *St. Martin's:* the St. Martin's theatre in London.
>
> *urban level:* same level as the rest of the town.
>
> *rubber:* a term used in some card games. Here the game would have been bridge.
>
> *Cheyne Gardens:* by the river Thames, on the Chelsea Embankment.
>
> *Metroland:* the country round London which could be reached by the Metropolitan Railway which ran underground most of the time, but came into the open as it approached country districts.
>
> *neo-Tudor:* modern buildings built in imitation Tudor style.
>
> *Penge:* an outer London suburb.
>
> *Commandment boards:* the painted boards behind the altar, found in seventeenth- and eighteenth-century churches.
>
> *aldermanic pomp:* ceremony attached to the office of an alderman, a town councillor who is next in dignity to the mayor.

p. 78.   SOUTH LONDON SKETCH, 1844

The Wandsworth of 1844 was part of London's countryside, with lanes and village inns. Today only Wandsworth and Clapham Commons are left of the original fields; the rest is covered with houses, and the great railway station of Clapham Junction stands near-by. But some of the lovely street names still tell of the Wandsworth of the past—Lavender Sweep, Sheepcote Lane, Mossbury Road, Longhedge Street, and many others.

p. 78.   WESTGATE-ON-SEA

Westgate is a late Victorian suburb of Margate, on the Kent coast. It is rather more exclusive than Margate and has red brick houses in wide, winding, tree-lined roads. Many of these houses are small private schools.

p. 79.   MARGATE, 1940

In 1940, during the first year of the Second World War, many people had left the big towns of the south-east coast. The children had been taken away to safer places, and no lights were permitted to show at night. This was called the 'black-out'. In Margate, John Betjeman looks from the balcony of the hotel he has known for years, into the blackness of the night, and remembers the Margate

he knew when, at the height of the season, all the entertainments were in full
swing and lights twinkled at night along the sea front.

thé dansant: a tea-time dance.

'Co-Optimists': a once-famous London concert party which dressed as
Pierrots and had seaside imitators.

Cliftonville: the next town along the coast—really an extension of
Margate.

p. 80.　　　　　　　　HENLEY-ON-THAMES

Another place recollected in wartime—Henley, the little Oxfordshire town on
the river Thames, famous for its boating and annual regatta.

prow-promoted gems: the bubbles made by ripples of water that fall away
from the prow of the boat as it goes along. (See verse I, last line.)

beefy ATS: the women of the Auxiliary Territorial Service—the women's
branch of the Army—were known as 'Ats'.

p. 81.　　　　　　　　WANTAGE BELLS

Wantage is the Berkshire town where John Betjeman lives. It lies at the foot
of the downs, and, in summer, flowers seem to be everywhere—in cottage
gardens, in hedgerows and along the banks of the stream. He feels no words
can express human gratitude for such beauty: only the church bells can ring
out eloquent thanks and praise.

p. 82.　　　　　　　　UPPER LAMBOURN

Over a high ridge of downs from Wantage lies the village of Lambourn, famous
for its race-horse training stables. The horses are ridden to exercise on practice
gallops on the downs, and strings of them come and go from the village through-
out the early hours of the day.

twenty-thousand: like the noise of twenty thousand little feet.

Carrara headstone: headstone made of white marble from Carrara in
Italy. It is often imported and used for gravestones.

he who trained . . . : one of the race-horse trainers.

sarsen stone: a sandstone boulder found on the chalk downs.

p. 83.　　　　　　　　HERTFORDSHIRE

This is a story of John Betjeman's youth. His father took him into Hertfordshire
to try to teach him how to shoot, but it was no good. John simply couldn't hold
a gun properly and finished up by shooting into the ground. His father was
pained by his clumsiness, but how much more pain he would have suffered
now, Betjeman thinks, if he could see what has happened to Hertfordshire
since then. New towns, factories, and houses have blotted out the former
countryside, and now it is only a continuation of London.

knickerbockered: knickerbockers were baggy trousers gathered in just
below the knee worn by sporting gentlemen.

syndicated shoots: land owned or rented by several people, any of whom may go and shoot birds and other game there during the shooting season—autumn and winter.

Lionel Edwards: (born 1878). An artist who specializes in sporting and hunting pictures with the rainy, grey skies of the English winter.

Landaulette: a form of early motor-car of which half the body would be open to the sky.

Brick boxes: modern houses.

p. 84.   NORFOLK

This part of Norfolk makes Betjeman remember his childhood and the time before he began to suffer the pains of growing up—like falling in love, and being let down and heart-broken. When did *that* all begin, he wonders? But here in Norfolk he used to have happy walks with his father, and return to their boat on the Broads where he would lie in his cabin at night and listen to the lap of the water against the sides. In those days he was carefree and innocent, and how wonderful it was!

Bure: a Norfolk river.

p. 85.   LAKE DISTRICT

At a lakeside café the poet is sitting and watching the lake, day-dreaming about a girl who goes to the top diving-board (he likes to imagine she's doing it specially for him) and plunges into the water. Yet the atmosphere of poetry and romance that dwells in the Lake District is somehow counter-blasted by the presence of H.P. Sauce and Heinz's ketchup and suggestions of very *un*romantic trippers.

p. 85.   ESSEX

This is another poem which looks back in time and sees a landscape of more beauty than is there today. A book of colour-plates shows John Betjeman the Essex of Edwardian days and reminds him of his own memories of the county when he was a boy.

Benfleet: a village a little way up the Thames Estuary from Southend.

Leigh-on-Sea: a town on the coast.

Matching Tye: an Essex village.

convoluted: twisted in design.

yarrow: a wild herb.

p. 87.   HARROW-ON-THE-HILL

Betjeman looks from Harrow-on-the-Hill, a north-west London suburb, in the dusk of an autumn evening and imagines he can see the Cornish coastline in the distance with the waves of the sea breaking upon it. In the half-light he sees a storm blowing up and a fleet of little trawlers hurrying round the headland to get into port before the storm breaks.

Wembley: the suburb to the south-east of Harrow-on-the-Hill.

Stadium: Wembley sports stadium.

estuary: in this sense, the estuary of the river Camel in north Cornwall, near Trebetherick, where John Betjeman went for holidays as a child.

Wealdstone: a part of Harrow below the hill.

Kenton: the suburb to the east of Harrow-on-the-Hill.

Perivale: the suburb to the south.

Pentire: Pentire Head, in north Cornwall, at the estuary of the river Camel.

Padstow : in north Cornwall—a little port town on the Camel estuary.

p. 87.   A LINCOLNSHIRE TALE

This tale with a ghostly theme is told by a Lincolnshire Archdeacon. The places in the poem are not real ones but as many Lincolnshire villages end in 'by', John Betjeman has made up his own names in Lincolnshire style. The Archdeacon travels in his carriage one evening down a long lane that leads past Speckleby Church and Rectory. He has never, in all his years of office, visited the Rector here, for he has heard of strange happenings and it is said that the Rector is mad. When the carriage reaches Speckleby Church, the Archdeacon's blood freezes for the pony suddenly falls dead and the church bell begins to toll. The manor house and park has long been deserted, but he gets out of the carriage and walks across the neglected grounds towards the church. The bell seems to draw him there against his will. As he stands by the tombstones, he sees the light of a moving taper shining from inside the church. At last he summons up courage to open the door. Inside, there is the smell of damp and decay and as he looks into the church, the bell stops tolling. Then he sees the Rector himself appear through a door and the sight so fills him with terror that he rushes away blindly into the night.

umber: dark, brownish-yellow pigment.

sign-painter's beasts: painted with the crude vigour of the old signboard of a village inn.

fell: terrible.

8. LATER SCHOOL

p. 93.   SUMMONED BY BELLS

John Betjeman went to public school when he was thirteen. The school was Marlborough in Wiltshire, which, like all public schools, allowed the boys themselves to form their own rules and customs, and for junior boys the first few years could be very miserable. This whole section is devoted to an extract from *Summoned by Bells* that describes John's life at Marlborough, and relates an incident that shows how a boy could be punished for some minor crime by his older schoolfellows. Times have changed since those days, of course, and what happened then would not be allowed to happen now.

The *Summoned by Bells* chapter begins with Betjeman lying in the bath with the steam swirling round him, letting his mind go back forty years to the school changing room which used to be filled with steam like this. Then he goes on with his memories of public school.

bat oil: the oil used on cricket bats.

Ut: a Latin preposition.

beaks: masters.

in Hall: dining-hall.

9. GROWING UP

p. 101.   SUMMONED BY BELLS

Still in pursuit of churches and architecture, John Betjeman comes eventually to the church of St. Ervan, Cornwall, where the Rector invites him to attend Evensong. During the service he sees all he wants to see of the church, but he doesn't go away immediately afterwards, for the Rector asks him in for a cup of tea. He talks to the boy about his religious beliefs and when he finds they are just as he suspected—'singing hymns and feeling warm and comfortable inside'—he lends him a book. John goes away and reads the book, and it sets him thinking about the deeper meaning of religion in a way that has never occurred to him before. He awakens to a different way of thinking, and from now on he is changed with this new realization; he is no longer a child. He is growing up and discovering his own beliefs.

St. Ervan: an early Cornish saint after whom the little thirteenth-century church is named.

red admirals: a kind of butterfly.

buddleia: a kind of shrub with lilac or yellow flowers.

apiary: place where bees are kept.

Rock: a village on the estuary of the river Camel opposite to Padstow.

Holy Grail: the cup from which Christ was believed to have drunk at the Last Supper, about which many legends have been told.

King Brychan: a Welsh king, many of whose children became priests and nuns in the Celtic Church and were later made into saints.

Celtic : this generally applies to Scots, Irish, Welsh and Cornish, but here it means only the Cornish Celts.

p. 103.   DISTANT VIEW OF A PROVINCIAL TOWN

The awakening of religious belief and uneasy feeling of conscience are reflected in this poem. The provincial town is Reading, Berkshire, which is one of the main railway stations between London and the West Country. Betjeman sees the spires that rise above the town—he knows all the churches—and sees the Great Western Railway, and somehow the two things stir deep feelings in him and make him feel remorse for his sins.

Popish: tending towards Roman Catholicism.

United Benefice: a church that once had a vicar of its own, but is now under the care of another church and its vicar.

unfrocked: his ecclesiastical office was taken away from him.

p. 104.   CHRISTMAS

This poem takes the theme of awakening religious belief even further. What is the meaning of Christmas? Do all the present-giving, the decorations, the feasting and carol-singing mean anything more than having a gay holiday? If they *do* mean something more, and the Baby born in a Bethlehem stable was the Son of God, come to save mankind, then the truth of this outshines all other truths, and man must live by it.

Advent: the four-week season before Christmas.

Tortoise stove: a make of metal stove used in churches.

Crimson Lake, Hooker's Green: names of colours.

classic towers: a poetic reference to some of the City churches.

shining ones: rich people.

Bread and Wine: the Church's sacrament of Holy Communion.